a memoir

ABOUT THE AUTHOR

From low-budget journeys as a student, to longer intervals living in Calabria, Switzerland, Vermont and New York, David Wickers has spent much of his life travelling. In his mid-thirties he discovered that, as a professional travel writer, he could be paid for his passion. For seventeen years he was Chief Travel Correspondent at the *Sunday Times* and is currently Travel Editor for *Good Housekeeping* magazine. He has received numerous awards, including being selected on four occasions as Travel Writer of the Year.

Back Stories is a collection of more than thirty highly personal traveller's tales, embracing adventure, comedy, disaster, romance, stupidity and a miscellany of mishaps, spanning more than five decades on the road. The cast of characters ranges from a prime minister to Father Christmas, a train robber to a horse called Big Mary, an Italian soothsayer to the head of the Fraud Squad.

David is married with three children, and lives in North London.

BACK STORIES

a memoir

DAVID WICKERS

The Book Guild Ltd

First published in Great Britain in 2021 by
The Book Guild Ltd
9 Priory Business Park
Wistow Road, Kibworth
Leicestershire, LE8 0RX
Freephone: 0800 999 2982
www.bookguild.co.uk
Email: info@bookguild.co.uk
Twitter: @bookguild

Copyright © 2021 David Wickers

The right of David Wickers to be identified as the author of this
work has been asserted by him in accordance with the
Copyright, Design and Patents Act 1988.

All rights reserved. No part of this publication may be
reproduced, transmitted, or stored in a retrieval system, in any form or by any means,
without permission in writing from the publisher, nor be otherwise circulated in
any form of binding or cover other than that in which it is published and without
a similar condition being imposed on the subsequent purchaser.

Typeset in 11pt Minion Pro

Printed on FSC accredited paper
Printed and bound in Great Britain by 4edge Limited

ISBN 978 1913913 526

British Library Cataloguing in Publication Data.
A catalogue record for this book is available from the British Library.

To Charlotte, Cesca, Maddy and Jonah,
with my love as always.

Contents

1	FIRST FORAY	1
2	EXTRA FAME	4
3	BORDER BOTHER	9
4	MOROCCO UNBOUND	12
5	AMERICAN DREAM	15
6	CALABRIATED	31
7	OFF PISTE	53
8	BIG MARY	55
9	THE BOOK THAT NEVER WAS	60
10	SANTA LIVES	68
11	SCENT OF A DOG	73
12	PISTE OFF	76
13	LOBSTER TALES	81
14	WASHED ASHORE	84
15	GOING WITH THE FLOW	87
16	VIRGIN SAILORS	93
17	THE WALK THAT NEVER WAS	98
18	IMPERFECT STORM	104

19	THE DEEP END	108
20	CAVE DWELLING	116
21	LEARNING CURVES	119
22	KIND HEARTS AND CASTANETS	122
23	PILGRIM'S PROGRESS	126
24	THE BIG CHOP	131
25	ROUND THE BEND	136
26	EAR MARKED	140
27	WORLD IN CRISIS	145
28	RONNIE IN RIO	150
29	ODD VIBRATIONS	153
30	GOING TO A BALL	158
31	PLAYING POLO	161
32	LORDS OF THE RING	164
33	TRAVEL MOMENTS	178

1

FIRST FORAY

Aside from a school trip to Brittany when I was thirteen and a week in Paris with just my best pal when I was fifteen, my first travel adventure didn't begin until 1963, with a six-month European journey in the 'Gap' between school and university.

I had saved around £350 by working as a pump attendant at a petrol station. Sometime, in early April, when I was a month shy of my eighteenth birthday, my dad drove me onto the Dover road and let me out at a lay-by where I started to hitchhike. We'd barely finished our goodbyes before a car stopped and I was off, leaving my dad looking a little stunned, as if a conjurer had spirited me away with a flick of a cloak.

My planned first stop was Paris. This also happened to be the destination of a girl, a UCH student nurse called Penny, whom I met on the ferry. She was travelling alone but had planned to stay with a friend who was studying at the Sorbonne. She gave me his address and said she was sure he'd be happy to put me up too. She then caught the train from Calais and I set off to hitch a ride.

It was late by the time I reached Paris, my last lift dropping me close to the Opera House. The evening was mild. I had a sleeping bag, so decided to bed down on top of its imposing front steps.

Nobody bothered me, nor did the police move me on, but nevertheless I slept badly, partly due to the hard stone floor but also the plummeting pre-dawn temperature. After warming up in a bar, I decided to make my way to the address of Penny's friend in the hopes of being offered a couch, or even a carpet, for a few days.

He, an English lad called Peter, could not have been more welcoming. Penny, who had slept on his sofa, had gone to buy baguettes. The coffee was brewing and Peter said that, if Penny was OK with the arrangement, she and I could both share his small living room. She agreed and we all enjoyed a few lyrical, *Jules et Jim*-ish days in the city.

One day, Parisian friends of Peter's parents invited all three of us to dinner at their home, a lavishly furnished, multi-roomed apartment in the swanky 16th arrondissement. I had no smart clothes but at least I still had a clean, Mum-ironed, collared shirt. I was, however, still embarrassingly underdressed for what turned out to be a rather formal occasion.

After drinks, including my very first Pernod (which reminded me of Milk of Magnesia), the guests, around twenty in total, were seated around a long dining table. The meal was prepared by a cook we never saw and served by a girl who smiled but didn't speak.

I sat between Penny and Peter at the far end of the table from Monsieur Le Host. He, Marcel, was rather intimidating, a man very used to sitting at the head of tables, directing conversations and expecting everyone, including his rather timid wife, to listen to his self-righteous ways of putting the world to rights.

At one point, Marcel fired a question directly at me, a hush descending on the rest of the table. He spoke, not unreasonably, in French and I struggled to reply. Roughly translated, the conversation went as follows:

He: *Are you sleeping with Penny?*

Me (spluttering in mid-sip of my glass of wine): *Oh, er, I will explain. I, we, is, are, sleeping on the floor.*

Or rather that's what I thought I'd said. In fact, I told him we were sleeping on the ceiling, confusing *plafond*, ceiling, with *planchard*, floor.

Everyone looked at me as if I was completely barmy, *un fou anglais*, but I quickly realised my mistake and, in my view rather suavely, delivered a very witty comeback.

Me: *Ah, that's because I am a fly, ho ho!*

Except, what I actually said was: 'That's because I am a handkerchief,' confusing *mouchoir* (fly) with *mouche* (handkerchief).

At least my two new friends thought it was hysterical. After a few uncomfortable seconds of silence, the guests resumed their babble and Monsieur Le Host ignored me for the rest of the evening.

2

EXTRA FAME

It was the very long summer of 1963, and I was spending six months, pre-university, hitchhiking around Europe. I had travelled from Paris to Biarritz, then to Lisbon, on to Algeciras in southern Spain and by ferry to Tangier, where I celebrated my eighteenth birthday with an omelette and wine in the company of an old Etonian who was staying in the same hostel. He said it was a shame I wasn't back in London as he could recommend somewhere on Cable Street where we could really have celebrated by 'scoring some excellent smack'.

Back into Spain, I then followed the Mediterranean coast as far as Brindisi in the heel of Italy, where I boarded a ferry to Greece. There was a friendly bunch of young travellers on board and I hooked up with three lads, all heading to Athens, two Brits and an Aussie called Wally who declared, as we coasted close to Albania, how he had imagined it would look: 'Flaming red, mate, not biscuit brown.'

We docked early in the port of Piraeus and decided to head

straight for the youth hostel in Athens. The plan was to check in, dump our bags, visit the Parthenon and find out whether we could, as we'd heard, sell blood to an agency in order to boost our rapidly dwindling finances.

While waiting in the hostel lobby, I noticed a couple of older men approach the receptionist, who then pointed in our direction. The two men came over, shook our hands and asked us if we would be interested in three days' paid work at a film studio. My first thought was that it was a scam, but they told us in some detail about the film, called *Kokkina Fanaria*, the Red Lanterns. Set in a fictional brothel in Piraeus, they needed a few extras to play the part of American sailors who were in port and 'having a good time with the girls'.

It was such an elaborate tale that we figured it must be true. The clincher for us was the offer of £3.50 a day, a lot in those days and a small fortune for us, plus lunch. Wally asked what the lunch would be. 'Chicken and chips,' one of the men replied, which settled it for Wally. We piled into a minivan for the short drive to the studios.

And so began my three-day career as a movie star. Or so we post-carded to friends and family back home. The set was a bar with a few tables and a spiral staircase leading to a balcony. A group of around twenty or so Greek actors and actresses, a good-looking lot, stood around, waiting, we presumed, for some sort of party to kick off. A couple of musicians were tuning up on a bouzouki and clarinet. Lots of crew were doing things to lights, cameras, sound poles and a tangled macrame of cables.

Our job, we were told, was to dance. That meant, in 1963, The Twist. Not that easy to perform to a bouzouki and clarinet, but for £3.50, chicken and chips we danced like devils and the filming began.

Day two was more of the same but with a highlight. The iconic sixties film star Melina Mercouri, then as internationally famous a Greek as Pythagoras or Onassis, came to visit the set, mainly to say hello and 'break a leg' to her good friend the director, and to meet and greet others – including us!

We were thrilled. She asked how long we'd been in Athens and I told her we'd only arrived the previous day. She wanted to know if we liked her beautiful city. I mentioned how our experience of Athens was currently on hold because we'd come straight to the studio on arrival. 'Oh, that's terrible,' she said. I explained that we felt it was an opportunity not to be missed and Wally told her it paid more than blood, an explanation she didn't quite follow. A newspaper photographer then took a photo of Melina and her new friends. I still have a copy. So, fortune and fame. And more chicken and chips.

That night we wined and dined in the lively old Plaka district. We celebrated our good luck, toasted our new friendships, raised glasses to those back home and staggered back to the hostel. The next morning, we managed to wake up just in time to make it to the minivan. Just. Had I known a rather demanding piece of acting was to be required of me, involving a dramatic plot twist, I might have laid off the sauce.

In a new scene, in the middle of the usual Twist routines, the gorgeous star of the movie appeared on the balcony and coolly surveyed the scene below. The director then approached me and explained, in broken English, how he wanted me to look at 'the beautiful girl above your head, finish your dancing, walk up the stairs. You, slowly, slowly, take the hand of Elena, with much pleasure, walk back with her down the stairs and you dance with her.' Oh yes, I can definitely do that. 'No problem,' I said.

The clapperboard clacked, the music resumed and I did my duty. There were (not my fault, I'm sure) three or four takes, but all seemed to be fine. So fine, I thought, that I considered asking for a pay rise, or double portions of lunch. It even crossed my mind to ask Elena to go for a drink after the filming, but, upon reflection, concluded that she was well above my daily £3.50 pay grade, let alone my looks grade.

After lunch we resumed our old dance routines, me with Elena. After a few more shots, there was a change in the action. A man, the co-star of the movie, entered the bar, walked through the crowd, elbowed everyone aside – including me, would you believe? – and stood right in front of Elena. He then smacked her right across the face! We were so genuinely shocked we had no problem acting a perfectly natural reaction, as you might have expected from the experienced thespians we were becoming.

During a break in the shooting, I asked one of the crew what that 'twist' in the plot had been about. He explained that the boyfriend had not realised that the love of his life was a hooker, and that was why she had been slapped.

Back to the grand finale, at least for our parts. At first this didn't go so well. The star couple, after the slap and the stunned silence, very quickly realised that, despite the revelations about her sex life, they were deeply in love and made it up with hugs and kisses. The director told the four of us to stand together, first to look very shocked, and then 'to be so very, very happy for the man and woman that we laugh with great joy'. A bit much to ask of me, I thought, having been suddenly jilted (interesting how quickly you can get into a part!), but it turned out that this was a bit much to ask of any of us.

The first thing that went wrong was when the director called 'action' and we realised that Wally wasn't around. A few seconds into our first attempt at laughing, the camera rolling, Wally wandered in from the lavatory asking when the filming was due to begin.

The director was not happy. Nor was he enamoured with our terrible attempts at laughing, convincingly, on cue. There were several takes, the tension mounting with each one, the 'laughter' becoming less and less believable.

As the filming dragged on, the studio became really hot, hardly surprising given the number of lights. Lots of the crew wore shorts, including the cameraman, who sat on a dolly, his legs splayed either side of the camera. Just as another take was about to be clapperboarded Wally happened to notice something. In a broad Aussie accent, he whispered, 'Check out the cameraman's tackle.' We looked and saw that his testicles had managed to slip outside the left leg of his shorts and were in full view of the four of us. We erupted into laughter. The director called, 'Wait!' but we couldn't, so he then called, 'Action', the clapperboard clacked and our final scene was recorded for posterity.

We got a big thank-you, collected our money and were driven back to the youth hostel. We were high. And rich. And, when we saw our photo with Melina in the next day's edition of the *Ta Nea* newspaper, indisputably famous.

I sent a postcard to my parents telling them about *The Red Lanterns* and asked them to look out for it in the unlikely event that it were to be distributed in the UK. One day, several weeks after I'd returned from the trip, they called me up at uni to say that the film was not only being screened at our local cinema but that there was a photo, a still, of me dancing, on display outside the cinema (common practice in the old days).

I went to see the film with a bunch of friends. They were utterly disrespectful, mocking my snazzy moves. And, somehow, they managed to laugh their heads off with no difficulty whatsoever.

3

BORDER BOTHER

One day, during a six-month, overland journey through Central and South America, I travelled by bus from Guayaquil in Ecuador to the border town of Huquillas, where I planned to cross into Peru and continue the adventure. Arriving at the frontier, I waited in line at the checkpoint along with other travellers, mostly backpackers who, like me, were working their way along the Pan American Highway.

One by one, we were asked to step into the office of a menacing, uniformed official, a two-pips-on-his-epaulette officer, who was sitting behind a desk. Two soldiers, carrying sub-machine guns, stood to one side.

'*Pasaporte*,' he demanded, propping his cigarette on the lip of an ashtray.

I handed over my, increasingly grubby-looking, document. He flicked it open, checked the photo, turned to a blank page and date stamped it with the word '*Salida*', meaning departure.

'*Cincos dolares!*'

Hang on. Exit visas are free, a fact confirmed by my South American Handbook, the backpackers' Bible.

'*Pero signor,*' I muttered. '*Non pago para salida. Es gratis.*'

'*Cincos dolares.*'

'*No signor, es gratis,*' I replied, rather aggressively.

Not a good move. The official took my passport, found another rubber stamp and overlaid '*Salida*' with one word, upper case, '*ANULADO*'. He thumped the stamp down again a second time. Twice '*ANULADO*'d'. He then opened the desk drawer, tossed the passport inside, closed it and looked me straight in the eye.

Now here's the really, not very clever, move. I walked over to his side of the desk, opened the drawer and took out the passport. The official, incandescent with rage, called over one of the soldiers and belted out a rapid, unfathomable order. The soldier grabbed the passport from my hand and gave it to the officer, who put it straight back into his draw and slammed it shut. The soldier then frog-marched me out of the office, past the line of gawping gringos, along the street and straight into the city's jail.

Oh dear. This was scary. The prison officer seemed rather bewildered and was clearly not too sure what he was supposed to do with me. While I stood in the open courtyard, surrounded only by a low wall topped by a tangle of barbed wire, I looked at the row of cells. Faces appeared at the tiny, open but barred, windows, two or three squeezing together at each one to watch the show. One tough and toothless prisoner put his hand through the bars and beckoned with sinister cries of, '*Eh, gringo. Venga a casa nostra. Muy bien. Es un palacio.*'

The prison officer put his hand on my arm and, without any sign of real force, 'encouraged' me to walk over to one of the cells. '*Aqui signor. Muy simpatico. Iz OK. You like.*'

Summoning some inner resolve, purely out of fear not bravado, I refused to go further. '*Non,*' I yelled. A bus had slowed down outside the compound allowing all the passengers to gawp at the goings-on. I turned to the onlookers and bellowed, '*Inocente! Inocente!*'

The next few minutes were confusing. The prison officer and the soldier talked, I continued shouting, more people stopped to look and the officer disappeared into his office. A couple of minutes later he stepped out, said something to the soldier, who then beckoned me with the barrel of his gun and pointed to the main entrance.

I had no idea where we were going but I figured anywhere must be better than being incarcerated with a bunch of gringo-hating local hoods, not knowing how long I was to be there, whether anyone would be notified of my predicament or whether I would have access to any form of representation.

The soldier led me straight back to where the sorry saga had begun. At least I was taken straight to the front of the gringo queue. When one fellow traveller stepped out of the office, clutching his passport and a wallet no doubt five dollars the lighter, I stepped in. The guard leaned towards the officer, said something quietly in his ear and then resumed his original position.

The officer took the passport from the drawer, opened the page, turned to a fresh one, took a drag of cigarette, balanced it on the side of the ashtray, had a sip of coffee and finally looked at me. I already had my five-dollar bill to hand. After a long, menacing pause, he spoke. '*Diez dolares.*'

Ten dollars!

'*Ah si. Si signor,*' I muttered, dug into my money belt for another five and handed over both notes. The officer then took his '*SALIDA*' stamp, banged it down onto the page and slid it across the desk. I took it, said, '*Muchos gracias,*' and set off for Peru.

4

MOROCCO UNBOUND

In the hippy, happy, heady days of the mid-seventies, four of us travelled across North Africa in a VW camper van. We drove through France to Italy, caught a ferry to Tunis and then made our way through Algeria and into Morocco.

We stopped in Ketama, in the high grasslands of Morocco's Rif mountains, a town famous as the commercial hub for the cultivators of marijuana. We were young, we were stupid and we bought a bagful, a bundle roughly the size of a grapefruit. We felt super cool.

As soon as the dealer had shaken hands and departed, we debated where we should hide our stash. It was a precautionary gesture, not really essential as we had no plans to smuggle it out of Africa. We secreted it in the back of the van, in a crevice between the side panel and a huge trunk that served not only for storing luggage and camping gear, but as the base that supported a mattress. We drove on.

On the main road out of town we spotted two men, in

uniform, standing on a hill and looking at the approaching vehicles. A police checkpoint! We were flagged down, made to get out of the van and told to form a line up against the VW's side door. The policemen peered into our eyes, looking for telltale signs of pupil dilation, which was fine as we hadn't yet had a chance to sample our wares. But, slowly, reality dawned. We had driven straight into a classic honey trap.

Pretty well every young European traveller who went to Ketama did so for one reason, to stock up on some of the finest weed. What better way to generate even more money for the local economy than for the seller, as soon as a transaction had taken place, to call his uniformed accomplices, give them the vehicle registration number and let them nab the naive buyers as they drove out of town?

We were, at the very least, in for a bribe that we would not be able to afford. At worst? Well, all sorts of scenarios ran through our frightened minds. After frisking our pockets, the policemen began methodically to search the vehicle, starting in the front, in the glove compartment, side pockets, under the seats. They then moved to the back and asked us to remove the mattress, take off the bed board that supported it, and to open the trunk. As I lifted the lid, I could clearly see the polythene bag. It was only a matter of time…

The meaner-looking of the duo told me to unload the trunk and pile everything at the side of the road. I complied, slowly, item by item: the sleeping bags, clothing, camping pots and pans, water containers, my typewriter… Each item was carefully examined and put to one side. The cop unzipped the typewriter case and peered inside before leaving it on the ground alongside our other belongings. I was about to take out the last of the items when he put his hand on my shoulder and asked why I had a typewriter.

I couldn't think of the French for writer, let alone 'aspiring, hope one day to become, writer'. I managed to stammer, '*Journaliste. Je suis un journaliste. Journalier. Presse.*'

'*Ah,*' the cop responded. '*Pourquoi vous n'avez pas dites que vous etes journaliste. Tout ca va. Allez vous en.*'

He beckoned his partner and the two of them sauntered off and resumed their vigil of approaching vehicles. We, shaking uncontrollably, reloaded the car and drove away. A mile or so later, with no signs of people or cars in front or in the mirror, we lobbed the bag into the bushes and made our way to Tangiers.

5

AMERICAN DREAM

As far as holiday jobs go, it was the dream ticket – taking a group of young American students on a two-month grand tour of Europe – and getting paid for the pleasure.

The job, as a tour leader for a company specialising in student travel, had been advertised in *Varsity*, the Cambridge student newspaper. I applied, filled in the form, which asked for details of previous travel experiences, language skills and the like, and was short-listed for a preliminary interview. This was to be conducted by two postgrad students who had previously led tours for the company and were now entrusted to sift through the initial list of hopefuls.

Although I'd included details of my extensive travels in between school and university, I had unashamedly exaggerated my language skills. I claimed to speak French and German, both of which were limited to minimal school requirements. I also included 'beginners' Spanish and 'enough to get by' in modern Greek, neither of which bore a kernel of truth.

I did wonder whether I should go through with what could well turn out to be a very embarrassing encounter, but I went ahead, posted the form and was summoned for an interview. After a few introductory pleasantries, with the two short-list sifters, the horror show began.

One began by asking me questions in French, which I was just able to answer, followed by German, which again I stumbled through. Then came Spanish. Luckily, I guessed the meaning of the question, which was where I'd previously visited in Spain. I replied by reeling off a number of towns pronounced, I brazenly felt, just like a native. It's hard to convey these answers on the page, but it involved a fair measure of lispy intonations as in my 'Barthelona', 'Valenthia' and 'Ibitha', plus a 'MaYorca' rather than a 'MaJorca'. I was also asked where I had stayed when travelling and I remembered '*habitaciones*' and '*hostals*', both very '*non mucho pesetas*' and '*muchos simpaticas*', I added for good measure.

We moved on. I feared what was about to come and did consider making an excuse and bolting. But instead of asking me a question in Greek, the interviewer simply said: 'What's your modern Greek like?' In English! Which rather suggested that he didn't speak a word of it either. I told him it was actually better than my Spanish, more or less on a par with my German.

I got through to the grand final, conducted in London by the two company directors. Since I had come this far on a rather bonkers quest, I felt there would be no shame in falling at the last hurdle. Both interviews, however, went surprisingly well. Not only was I offered a tour but the star itinerary, a ten-weeker designed to scoop up eleven different countries.

Fast forward to early summer. A day before my group was due to arrive at Heathrow, I checked into their London hotel, just off Tottenham Court Road, and then went to the company's office for a three-hour briefing. It was delivered, at great speed, by the intimidating MD, who barely paused in his breakdown of the day-to-day schedule. The bones of the itinerary were fleshed out by reams of background information, about guides and transfers, about trains, planes, coaches and ferries, about vouchers I would need for meals and hotels, museums we were scheduled to visit and several restaurants which had already been pre-booked.

I scribbled away, occasionally summing up the courage to interrupt with a question. I was particularly careful to understand the procedure for boarding the ship in Venice that was to carry us down the Adriatic to Greece. It involved arranging to hire a barge to transfer all the suitcases from the hotel on the Lido island, across the lagoon to the quayside near St Mark's, then finding porters who would load them on board. The tour leader then meets up with the group in the afternoon and escorts everyone to the ship. However, word had filtered through that during the previous summer, one of the tour leaders had mistakenly loaded the group's luggage onto the wrong ship, leaving his charges with no clean clothing or toiletries until they docked in Piraeus three days later.

Back to London. The following day, I met my group at Heathrow. There were twenty-two women and six men, aged between seventeen and nineteen, the oldest just two years younger than me. One had already arrived and had been visiting an aunt in Wales, another was due to arrive the following day. Many had been given the trip, which in today's money would probably cost around £10,000, as a high school graduation present by their parents or, more often, loving grandparents.

We coached into central London. I said a few words by way of welcome and reeled off a few housekeeping notes. Many of my flock, however, had nodded off from the combined effects of jet lag and their overnight flight.

There was nothing arranged for the rest of the day. I made a few suggestions and told everyone to meet in the hotel lobby the following morning for their full-day city tour. I spent the rest of my day back at the office, for a follow-up briefing and to collect documents, including a wad of travellers' cheques and petty cash to cover tips and incidentals. I read through the itinerary a few more times, resolving to stay at least three or four days ahead of the schedule, and went to bed early, hoping for several hours of deep sleep so that I would be fully alert in the morning.

At around 3am my bedside phone rang. The gist of the conversation went as follows:

Hello.

Hello. Sorry to bother you, sir, but am I speaking to 'Dave'?

Yes, well, David, that is. Who's calling? It is three in the morning…

Well, Dave, we have a bit of a problem. This is PC Saunders from Tottenham Court Road police station. We've had to take a young American chappie called 'Chip', a Chip Walker, into custody and he insists we speak to you.

Oh yes, Walker. He's one of a group of American students that I'm looking after. They only flew in yesterday morning. What on earth's happened?

Well, sir, Dave, it's a rather serious matter. The gentleman, Chip, had clearly had rather a skinful. We found him an hour or so ago, fast asleep on a sofa in the front window of a furniture store. It seems he smashed the window, stepped inside and then collapsed on the sofa. It's a wonder he hadn't severed an artery in the process.

My God!

I'm afraid we'll have to keep him here. He will no doubt have to appear in court, before a magistrate. We do have his passport – it was in his pocket – and we'll be contacting the American Embassy first thing in the morning, and his parents, but I thought we should follow up on his request that we contact you. Presumably you'll need to call your head office and explain what's happened.

I did make those calls and, to cut a long story short, Chip was repatriated to the USA after a few days as a guest of HM government. One down, but still one to come, a girl called Brett.

One of the strong messages conveyed in my briefing with the MD was that under no circumstances was there to be any 'intimate, unprofessional relationships' between tour leaders and their students. I also knew, within a very short space of time, this was going to be unsustainable.

The only other unscripted event in London was my deciding to abandon three girls at Westminster Abbey. Just before we disembarked on Parliament Square, I told everyone when and where to board the coach after the visit, emphasising the need to be bang on time because of parking restrictions. After waiting ten minutes, we were told to move on by a policeman, so set off minus the trio. Although it was a tough call, and I did feel sorry for the girls, it was probably a good message to convey early on in the tour. When I caught up with them later they had, thankfully, taken things in their stride and bore no ill feelings towards their fuhrer.

From London we flew first to Amsterdam. I didn't let on that it was the first time I'd ever been on a plane. My tour-leader credentials would have taken a serious dive if my students, all of them experienced air travellers, knew I was a virgin flyer.

We travelled on, north to Scandinavia, south through Germany where, in Munich, one of the girls fell madly in love with a GI and had to be shoehorned back onto the tour with the help of a phone call from an anxious aunt in Arizona, then Austria, through Sound of Music countryside, to Switzerland. In Lucerne I had been advised, by a seasoned tour leader, to go round to the back entrance of one of the big watch and jewellery stores, leave a list of all my students, and return later to collect a sealed envelope. It was stuffed with Swiss francs; the group had spent a fortune and my commission was enormous.

We drove on to Venice, where I did put the luggage on the right ship, and sailed down the Adriatic to Piraeus. We visited the Parthenon and toured the Peloponnese before taking the ferry back to Brindisi in the heel of Italy. We coached north, nipping across to Capri, explored Pompeii and then rounded the coast to Monaco, Nice, into Spain and finally to Lisbon.

Throughout the ten weeks, the relationship between Brett and I flourished. Luckily everyone loved Brett too, so we didn't bother hiding our romance (unlike the following year, on a Russian tour, when a far less significant affair impacted very badly on the group's *esprit de corps*).

The final dinner was a lively but a sad occasion, made all the more miserable by the company's choice of a Fado restaurant where musicians performed Portugal's famously melancholic music. There was a sour note too. The group had bought me a leather wallet in which they had put a US$100 note, a huge sum in the 1960s. It was stolen from my hotel room while we were having dinner.

The last I saw of Brett, for several months, was watching her slowly climb the boarding steps onto the TAP airline bound for New York where most of the group were connecting onto domestic flights, including hers to Boston.

Fast forward to the following summer, the intervening time peppered with lots of wonderful letters winging their way between Cambridge and Boston. Because my tour had been deemed a great success by the company directors, I was offered a second tour, called 'To Russia with Love'. Since I had the upper hand in deciding whether to take it, I asked the MD if, were I to do it, the company would throw in a one-way ticket to New York. He agreed.

Although my relationship with the group was problematic, the tour was very exciting. It was a time when Russia, the USSR, lay heavily under the communist yoke. We were escorted throughout, from Leningrad to Moscow and on south to Kiev and Odessa, both by an Intourist guide and a man in a mac who never spoke a word. I was forbidden to communicate with head office, or anyone else outside the country, so when we eventually arrived in Istanbul, travelling by ship over the Black Sea and down the Bosphorus, I was greeted by a telegram from the MD saying, 'COME IN FROM THE COLD? IMMEDIATE DEBRIEF, PLEASE.'

Shortly after the Russian group returned, I flew to New York on my free ticket, then immediately made my way to the Port Authority bus terminal and caught a late-night Greyhound to Boston. It was not the most relaxing of journeys. I sat next to a seemingly quiet, bespectacled old lady, a granny straight out of central castings. Half-way into the ride, in the dark interior with everyone trying their best to sleep, she suddenly screamed, 'Help, help, he's raping me.' She stood up, pointed her gnarled finger at me and yelled, 'Driver, driver, help. Stop the bus. It's him.'

The driver pulled onto the hard shoulder of the freeway, got out of his seat and worked his way back to where I was sitting, the woman still standing over me. He quickly, and astutely, assessed the situation, told the woman to shut up and go to sleep, and told me to find another seat.

The rest of the journey was uneventful and I arrived in Boston around five in the morning, the sky just beginning to lighten. It was too early to make a phone call, so I sat in the bus station, a gathering spot for all species of waifs and strays, carefully avoiding all eye contact.

I called Brett's house around 7am and was warmly greeted by her mother. She woke Brett, who came to the bus station to collect me.

Although we had both long yearned for this moment, we didn't have an easy time. Months had passed and, rather than rekindling the passions of the previous summer, things felt awkward. The family had arranged a poolside BBQ in the afternoon for lots of family and friends, including Brett's sister, her Peace Corps boyfriend and an old boyfriend of Brett's called James who had remained a friend and was definitely not best pleased to see me.

Brett and I had planned to spend a few days in Boston and take up an offer from Brett's dad, an orthodontist, to drive his cool sports car on a trip along the coast of Maine. But, since there was an uncomfortable feeling of detachment between us, I felt it better for both of us if I were to move on.

I had already given the family's telephone number to another tour leader, Jack, who had done a similar US ticket deal with the student travel company and had flown out to New York a few days before me. Coincidentally, the day I decided to leave Boston, he rang. A company that recruits drivers to deliver vehicles on behalf of owners who want to relocate but don't want the hassle of driving long distances, had offered him a car, a VW Beetle, which was destined for San Francisco. He'd been given eight days to cross the country and asked if I'd like to join him? I agreed and returned to NYC the next day, feeling an emotional wreck but excited by the prospect of my first US road trip.

The journey was a great adventure. Not only did transporting the car make the trip affordable, but we were also able to arrange stays with several of our previous tour members who were conveniently scattered right across the country. After spending lots of time in San Francisco, we later managed to get hold of another car, a snazzy sports Pontiac Le Mans, whose owner wanted it driven all the way back to the east coast. This time we took a more southerly route and were able to stay with a different batch of students.

By the time we reached New York we were both flat broke and urgently needing to find work in order to pay for our flights back to the UK. We had one very hopeful contact. A girl on one of Jack's previous tours lived in New York. Her trip had been paid for by her grandfather, Leonard Milsom, who happened to own two of the largest travel companies in the US, headquartered in midtown Manhattan. She arranged for Jack and me to meet him, in his office, in the hope of picking up some temporary menial work, filing documents, perhaps, or helping out in the company's mail room.

Milsom had an enormous, swanky suite of offices, his own roost having corner windows which looked down and along

Madison Avenue. It was prime *Mad Men* territory. Milsom was welcoming, introduced us to his number two, Harry, ordered coffee and asked us about our travels, both as student tour leaders and our recent roamings around the US. It did feel rather like an interview and I was delighted when, at last, he uttered the magic words: 'Hey, how would you boys like to work for me?'

We, of course, readily agreed, conveying that we really didn't mind what we did. Both Milsom and Harry laughed and asked whether we had fully grasped what was on the table. Milsom continued. 'What I mean, boys, is that I'd like to offer you proper jobs, long term. I'm afraid I've got to shoot off to a meeting, but if the idea sounds interesting, Harry here will flesh out some of the details. Sound good?'

Sound good? It sounded as if it could be absolutely, bloody marvellous. We shook hands with Milsom and then Harry explained the corporate make-up. It comprised two main travel divisions but how they were now looking to create, even before we showed up on the scene, a third, targeted at students, which they felt was going to be the next big thing in travel. Since we had first-hand knowledge of that side of the business, we would be ideal candidates to set up, market and run a student programme.

We agreed. We especially, doubly, trebly, agreed when Harry offered us an obscene amount of money which, in order to circumvent US rules regarding work permits, would be paid directly into a numbered Swiss bank account. Everything that we spent in New York, on accommodation, meals, going out and about, and so on, we could claim as expenses.

We were given our own office, also overlooking Madison Avenue, and a PA called Arlene. We checked into a hotel for a couple of weeks, then rented an apartment close to the old Pan Am building which sat astride Park Avenue. We went out most nights, claimed restaurants and bar bills, club entrances and taxis, simply handing over receipts at the end of each week to a very suspicious finance manager. Since winter was approaching, we also bought, and claimed, overcoats and other cosy items of clothing.

We did what we had agreed to do and everyone was delighted. We created the student travel wing, which we called Student Wheels Abroad, initially designing eight European tours, similar to the ones we had previously led. Once approved, the plan was for Jack to stay on in New York and take care of sales and marketing while I would be dispatched to Lucerne, Switzerland, where the operations of the other two, very different, travel divisions were based. My job was to plan and organise the tours, to contract hotels, book coaches, trains and ferries, arrange sightseeing, recruit tour leaders… in fact almost everything except for air ticketing, a task performed by an in-house airline guru.

I flew to Switzerland via London, spending a few days seeing my mum and dad and catching up with friends. In Lucerne, I checked into a hotel and went to the office, which stood on a hill overlooking the town. One of the travel divisions, Seven Wonders Travel, was headed by another Englishman, John Dennis-Browne.

John, Johnny, lived with Marsha, his American wife, in a rather grand house in a tiny village outside town, whose back garden was lapped by the waters of Lake Lucerne. We became friends. After a couple of weeks, they suggested that I might prefer to share their house rather than live in a hotel. I readily agreed.

And so began a magical chapter. I moved into the house and asked Brett if she wanted to join me. She agreed, but first wanted to go to Israel, to work on a kibbutz for a couple of months, and then come to Switzerland.

On a quick trip back to London, I bought a TR4A and drove it back to Switzerland. I loved the journey, except for the moment when its detachable hard top managed to detach itself while I was belting along a German autobahn. Luckily, it gusted onto the hard shoulder and I sheepishly retrieved it without any nasty consequences.

Everyday, Johnny and I would race the dozen or so miles from house to office (he had a Porsche!). At home, at the weekends, we threw parties, went water-skiing from the wall at the end of the garden, enjoyed wonderful walks in the mountains and explored other parts of the country. I also started going out with one of the girls from the office, Luzi.

One day, after the Wheels tour programme had been fully curated, the brochures printed and distributed in the US, news reached us that President Johnson, in a move to strengthen the US balance of payments, proposed to introduce a tax on Americans travelling abroad. In the end, his scheme was never implemented but the impact on our embryonic student travel company was likely to be disastrous. I was asked to return to New York for 'urgent discussions'.

Before I even arrived at the office, Milsom and the other directors had decided that our mission was to be aborted. Jack had already been thanked for his services and was never seen again. I imagined I would also be given the chop and had been considering a big trip to South America, spending some of my newly accumulated wealth. The day after I arrived in New York, I was invited to a meeting with Milsom.

Milsom was surprisingly friendly, considering he was about to bid me farewell. This conversation went as follows.

Milsom: *David, good to see you. Sorry to haul you back from Switzerland at such short notice.*

Me: *That's fine. Always happy to visit New York.*

Milsom: *Well, I guess you've heard the bad news about Student Wheels?*

Me: *I have. Such a shame. I'm sure it would have been a great success at any other time.*

Milsom: *I'm sure too, but this is definitely not the time to launch a new travel company. However, moving on…*

Me: *Yes, I was thinking, maybe South America—*

Milsom: *How old are you, David?*

Me: *Twenty-three.*

Milsom: *Twenty-three, eh? David Wickers, twenty-three years old, Vice President of Seven Wonders Travel. How does that sound to you?*

Me: *I don't understand.*

Milsom: *We want you to take over and head up the company's operations in Lucerne.*

Me: *But that's what Johnny does.*

Milsom: *Can we talk in confidence, David?*

Me: *Sure.*

Milsom: *The simple fact of the matter is that we no longer believe Johnny's the right fit for the company. Too reckless. Out of control. We need to keep a much tighter rein on the operations side of the business. We believe it's time for a change.*

Me: *But have you discussed this with Johnny? I only saw him a couple of days ago and he didn't mention anything about it.*

Milsom: *That's because he doesn't know anything about it. We wanted to sound you out first. We'd like you to go back to Switzerland. We'll tell Johnny how we appreciate how busy he is, how he could no doubt do with some help and how you are suddenly free to work for Seven Wonders. But while, ostensibly, the idea is for you to absorb some of his work-load, the real purpose of sending you there is to find out as much as you can about the company's operations. We'll let Johnny know that you're coming and, as soon as you feel able to take over, we'll quietly let Johnny go. Sound good?*

Me: *Well, yes, but—*

Milsom: *OK, that's settled. We'll talk more but, meantime, hop on the next plane back to the land of the cuckoo clock and let's get things moving.*

I flew to Zurich, picked up my car from the airport and drove to Lucerne. I walked straight into the office and Johnny gave me a warm welcome. He'd had a call from New York, explaining why I was being dispatched to Switzerland, and he had told them he was delighted by the idea of my joining Seven Wonders. I explained how that was not quite the full story.

I told Johnny everything. How I'd really been sent on an 'undercover assignment' and that the company had already written his obituary. We decided that we would carry on, diligently running the company as before, and I would continue to stall by telling New York that I wasn't quite ready to take over. We figured they would, eventually, become so frustrated by the slow progress and give Johnny the sack anyway, at which point I would also quit and we'd both ride off into the sunset.

It was business as usual for the following two or three months. We enjoyed the house by the lake and I did a fair amount of travelling. Every two or three weeks, Harry the side kick would ring up from New York. First he would ask, in a soft voice, if I was able to talk freely, which of course I always was, even when Johnny was standing right beside me. He would then ask how everything was going and whether I was ready to take the helm. My usual response was to claim that I needed another two or three weeks, as I was still trying to get to grips with some of the more complicated issues, such as our hotel contracts, or the weekly charter flight we operated between London and Rome, details of which, I maintained, were tricky to get hold of without arousing Johnny's suspicion.

Gradually New York became not only increasingly irritated but more than a little suspicious. One time – it was early March – they called when I was away in Israel, which I'll come back to later. Without warning, Harry and a couple of key New York execs flew to Switzerland and turned up unannounced at the Lucerne office.

Johnny explained that I was in Tel Aviv on company business, which was mostly true, but somehow they sussed what was going on and told him that I would be immediately sacked on my return. The execution was to be carried out by Mr Wainwright, a mean-spirited Brit who ran the other main travel division and was the most senior in the Swiss hierarchy.

In a complete reversal of our planned scenario, in which Johnny gets the sack and I throw in the towel, Johnny told the

New Yorkers that, if they sacked me, he would quit. And that's exactly what happened,

Being still in the days of feeble and horrendously expensive international telecommunications, I had no idea that all this had been going on while I was in Israel. As soon as I finished company business (two of our itineraries included Israel), I rented a car and drove to Haifa, checked into a hotel, the Dan Carmel, and then went straight to a kibbutz called Ein Hashofet, roughly thirty kilometres from the city, where Brett was living.

We fell into each other's arms, old passions immediately reignited despite the months apart. But there was a problem. A large truck drove up as we were in mid-embrace and a guy leaned out of the window, looking most put out by what he saw. Brett unhitched herself and walked up to the truck. She and the guy spoke for a while – I could not hear what was being said – and she returned to where I was standing. She was, she explained, having a relationship with the guy but suggested that I went back to Haifa and she would come to the Dan Carmel that evening, and stay with me for a few days. We talked about Switzerland, but I also explained I was involved with someone else. I left the kibbutz and drove back to Haifa.

I had bought four hundred duty-free Marlboro at Zurich airport, a brand we both smoked. At 8pm, before going down to the hotel foyer, to be there when Brett arrived, I constructed a tower of the cigarette packs.

The foyer was heaving and there were armed security guards all over the place. As I stood to one side, Ben Gurion, founder and first Prime Minister of Israel, arrived to rapturous cheers and applause from the crowd. He was led away, the crowd thinned, but there was no sign of Brett. I waited, then went into the restaurant to eat. At around 11pm I went back to the room to find my tower of Marlboro had ominously collapsed.

I flew back from Tel Aviv to Zurich in late March, picked up my car and drove straight to our house on the lake to find a note pinned up in the kitchen. 'Dear David. The Ides of March have come and gone. You've been sacked and I martyred in your cause. Marsha and I are off to Scotland, then Greece. Don't give anyone any documents. Johnny.'

The next day I drove to the office. Instead of being greeted with a sympathetic smile and words of condolence from Wainwright, he simply said, 'I want your company charge cards. Now!' I had two, one for car rentals and one for airline tickets. I told him I'd left them at the house and I would, after emptying my desk, drive back and get them. I asked how he planned to settle my outstanding expenses from my last two work trips, which I placed on his desk. He said, 'You can forget all about those.'

Instead of returning to the house, I drove back to Zurich airport and went to the TWA airline sales desk. I bought an open-dated, return ticket to Boston. The cost was still shy of what I was owed. I asked the price of a round trip London to Dublin ticket, a place I'd always wanted to visit. I could afford two and still be within my limit. I bought two.

I drove back to Lucerne, put the charge cards on Wainwright's desk and said not to worry about the money the company owed me as all debts were settled. I then waited for Luzi to finish her day and we drove back to the house and opened a bottle of champagne.

I spent a week walking in the mountains with Luzi and then returned to London. Having anticipated that the American adventure couldn't possibly last forever, I had already started to pay for a room in a flat in Hampstead, one that was being rented by a couple of friends, and moved straight in.

A short while later I received a letter from Brett. She explained how, on the night she had failed to turn up at the Dan Carmel, she had packed her bags and ordered a taxi to collect her from the kibbutz. When it arrived, the guy she was seeing ran out, grabbed her by the arm and paid off the taxi. His friends and family also joined in the action. She remained at the kibbutz for a few more days and then fled, flying back to Boston. She asked me to come to the US.

A couple of months later I decided to fly to Boston, using my TWA ticket. Friends drove me to Heathrow and I left them in a cafe while I went to check in. At the TWA desk, the agent looked carefully at my ticket and asked me if I wouldn't mind coming back to the desk five minutes later. She said she needed to check something with her supervisor.

I went over to my friends and must have looked as terrified as I felt. They knew the back story to the ticket and we discussed whether we should all get straight back in the car and forget the whole thing, imagining that TWA, at that very moment, could well be on the phone to airport security, even the Fraud Squad.

But I knew I had done nothing criminal, had merely taken what was rightfully mine, and somewhere I still had all the paperwork and receipts to prove my innocence if it ever came to a court case. Nervously, I went back to the TWA desk. 'Sorry about that, Mr Wickers,' the agent said. 'Our flight is rather full today, so we've put you in first class. Have a wonderful flight.'

6

CALABRIATED

In the seventies I spent a year living in the forested foothills of the Sila mountains of Calabria, deep in the raw, poor foot of the Italian boot. My home, just outside a village called Amaroni (pop 1,800), was a simple room in a tiny, rough old farmhouse which belonged to Luigi Devito, a wiry, passionate, charming but cantankerous old man. Here's how I came to be there.

Some two years prior to going I had been working in the pretty Swiss town of Lucerne for an American travel company (a tale told on page 15 in this collection). Vreni Jencarelli, a Swiss girl, worked as a secretary to one of the bosses. She was married to Franco, an Italian who grew up in Amaroni.

Long neglected by Rome in favour of Italy's northern economic powerhouse, Calabria was one of Italy's most impoverished regions. Franco, along with other young men from the village, had left home in his teens to find work abroad and was now employed in the Lucerne factory of the ski manufacturer Rossignol. We became good friends and I spent many happy evenings at their flat. They also often came to visit me in a house I shared with Johnny, Marsha and Luzi, bang on the shores of Lake Lucerne in a village called Buochs.

One evening Franco showed me a Super 8 film he had made of Amaroni. I was utterly enthralled by the portrayal of a life so alien to anything I had ever experienced, a contrasting world of poverty and laughter, of grey, sombre buildings and spectacular scenery. His film also showed an annual *festa* when an effigy of the patron Santa Barbara was paraded along the main street, of locals working in the fields or at play on a nearby beach. But there was one story that Franco told, rather than showed, that was even more intriguing than the shaky, fuzzy-edged Kodachrome images.

It was a tale about an Amaroni man who was supposedly gifted with the ability to predict people's deaths. At the time of the full moon, the soothsayer would enter a trance-like, catatonic state. His blood, Franco explained, would seep through the pores in his palms and, raising his eyes to heaven, he would declare, with fiery conviction, the name of the villager next in line for the grim reaper.

The soothsayer never named names but made more sweeping predictions, along such lines as 'a man who wears a hat will be dead by the end of the month'. His words would inundate the village like a tidal bore. Despite the power that the church held in the community, within a matter of hours none of the men would be seen wearing a hat, at least until the following full moon. The next accompanying prediction would, of course, have nothing to do with hats but another behavioural trait that would spell mortality for some poor soul.

Such were the social demographics of Amaroni, with its disproportionate number of old men, that the odds were high on at least someone dying every four or five weeks. Whatever the cause of death, hindsight could be cleverly reshaped in support of the prediction and so reinforce the status of the old supernaturalist. If, for example, a man died who was not wearing a hat, people would swear that he was most definitely seen wearing one earlier on that fateful day he died, or that the wind had blown it off, or perhaps he'd left it on the counter of the bar.

I resolved to go to the village, immerse myself in this remarkable world and, hopefully, take photographs or write about the soothsayer. But I had to leave Switzerland sooner than planned – again a story detailed in another chapter – and had decided, for a host of reasons, to spend a few months travelling around South America. It was only towards the end of that trip, with some money left over from previous employment, that I knew the place I most wanted to go. Calabria.

I wrote to Franco from Brazil to ask whether he thought there was any possibility of my being able to spend some time in the village. Franco contacted both his father and a cousin, both of whom responded with great enthusiasm. There were no details, other than Franco telling me that everything would be fine, I'd be taken care of. All I had to do was turn up and introduce myself.

A few weeks later, in early April, I loaded up my newly acquired car, an old, tetchy, Fiat 600, and drove from London to Calabria.

The journey was slow, 600cc slow, and mostly uneventful apart from a time on the *autostrada* when hot brown liquid, not unlike freshly brewed tea, began to pour from somewhere below the steering wheel onto my feet. It came from a ruptured aneurysm on the radiator hose. Despite the vehicle being crocked and having to be piggy-backed off the highway on a pick-up summoned from a local garage, I still remember feeling outraged at having to pay the exit toll, especially when the mechanic also had to pay, a fee that, of course, appeared on the final bill.

When I finally reached Amaroni it was almost dark and the weather was foul. The village, never a pretty sight even under a blazing sun, looked menacing. I parked and went into a bar to ask where I could find Signor Jencarelli (Franco had forgotten to give me an address). An old gent stood up from one of the tables, waved me over, ordered me a glass of wine and sat me down. 'I am Jencarelli, the father of Franco,' he declared. We clinked glasses.

Despite having had a few Italian audio lessons at a language lab back in the UK, I could barely understand what he was saying, the local dialect, further slurred by wine, being rather unfathomable. I began to feel I might have made a big mistake and considered coming up with some excuse for having to move on, but a second glass of wine arrived, maybe the fourth or fifth for Jencarelli. Other old men came over and introduced themselves, and, a couple of hours later, we all left the bar and walked unsteadily, in a rag-tag procession, to Casa Jencarelli.

I met Franco's mother, who immediately scolded her husband for leading me astray and asked if I was hungry. A dish of pasta and another glass of wine later, I was shown a spare room with a tiny bed beneath a crucifix.

Welcoming as the Jencarellis were, there was no way I wanted to stay in Amaroni for more than a night or two, let alone the planned few months. Everything was gloomy and rather melancholic. But, by morning, the rain had passed and the sun was beaming through my window. I could smell the coffee percolating on the stove and, in a dramatic about-turn of emotions, I was up for whatever Amaroni threw at me.

I joined the Jencarellis in their kitchen over coffee (me) and beer (Dad). He raised the glass and passed on his golden rule for good living: '*Solo birra avanti mezzogiorno, solo vino nel pomeriggio e la sera,*' he declared ('only beer in the morning, only wine in the afternoon and evening').

Salvatore was sent for, a lovely man with silver hair and a cheeky smile in his eyes. He had spent a few years living in South Mimms in North London, where a small community of

Amaronese had taken root. He spoke enough English for me to grasp the gist of what was going to happen to me.

First, I was to wait for 'the cousin'. Then we would all go into the mountains and meet Luigi. There would be a room. Salvatore also gave an update on the soothsayer. He had died the previous month. Nobody seemed to know whether he had predicted his own demise. Or if he was wearing a hat.

The cousin, Rocco, arrived, a softly spoken, diffident man, one of the few who was able to find work locally, as a builder, without have to join the diaspora abroad like Franco. With the scantiest of explanations, Rocco and I, plus Salvatore and Jencarelli, set off up the main street, past the church and a couple of bars, one being where Jencarelli peeled off from the procession and disappeared through a red plastic fly curtain with a wave and a see-you-later.

His place was soon taken by Barbara, cousin Rocco's wife, wearing a pinny on which she wiped her floury hands before shaking mine. We crossed a bridge over a trickle of a river and headed out of the village. Like the Pied Piper, we had somehow managed to attract a small posse of giggling children who seemed fascinated by the presence of an 'Inglese' in their village.

After about 500 yards the path forked, one going steeply down to what I later discovered to be a natural spring, the other rising up past a series of cultivated terraces to a *casetta*, a rendered breeze block building with a corrugated tin roof. There, at its gate made from branches of chestnut, stood Luigi Devito. He smiled, shook hands, spoke to Rocco, cut a rose from a bush and handed it to me. We then went inside.

Gradually it dawned that this was to be my home. The front door opened onto a tiny lobby, where there were two pairs of boots, a shotgun, a thick coat and a couple of green, glass flagons full of wine. Straight ahead was the kitchen with just a two-hob propane gas stove, an open fire, pots and pans, and a shelf with rows of empty brown beer bottles.

To the left was a room with a table, chairs, a single bed, a couple of sacks of flour, various jars, more beer bottles – filled, I later found out, with tomato sauce – and a large, lovely, shy and beaming lady called Anna Marie, Luigi's wife, who immediately asked if I'd eaten. To the right was a room with a bare metal spring bed base, a small cupboard, a single chair, a table that swayed on its legs and unpainted concrete walls. This was to be my room. The fourth room, next to mine but with a separate entrance, belonged to Estrella, the cow.

There were more people to meet. Martina, Luigi's daughter-in-law, was dark-skinned with beautiful black, laughing eyes. She was dressed entirely in black, including a headscarf, forever in mourning after the death of her father several years previously. She had two children, four-year-old Little Luigi, dark like his mother, and two-year-old Little Anna Marie, who took several days before daring to appear from behind her mother's legs. Martina's husband, Domenico, Luigi's son and the kids' father, lived and worked in Germany and would not be returning to Amaroni until August, the same month that Franco, Vreni and their two children, Miriam and Marco, would also be coming, along with a brigade of young village men, other *gastarbeitern* or 'guest workers' from factories in Germany and Switzerland.

Things happened fast. I spent the second night back with Franco's parents. The next day I drove first to the nearest, medium-size town, Girifalco, to buy all sorts of essentials including food and wine. On my return, I parked in the main square and joined a convoy of all the Devitos, who had a house in the village, who helped carry my wares to the *casetta*.

Walking in single file along the narrow footpath, we must have looked like a whacky scene from a Fellini movie. On her head, Anna Marie carried a rolled-up mattress stuffed with dried wheat stalks. This was my bed (on another occasion she even carried a full-size fridge freezer all the way from the village). Martina had a gas cylinder on hers, to fuel a hob.

I carried a couple of suitcases from the Fiat, Luigi a sack of leftovers from their previous evening meal for the animals, Little Luigi a stick and Anna Marie Piccola, her doll.

By the time we reached the *casetta* my room had already been whitewashed and the bare wires that had poked down from the ceiling were now attached to a bulb. I helped carry the mattress in and laid it on the springs. It was beginning to look just a little bit liveable.

A pattern to Amaroni days gradually evolved. Sometimes Luigi would spend the night in the *casetta*, often with Little Luigi (whom I called 'Signor Si' just to distinguish between the two), squeezed into their single bed. But mostly the entire family would sleep in their modest village house, leaving me for the night in the company of Estrella and Bruno, the dog, a sleek, friendly, caramel-coloured mongrel.

Each morning, after a rousing chorus of Estrella mooings, chicken clucking, cockerel roostering, guinea pig squeaking, doves a'cooing and turkey warblings, a Noah's Ark in quadraphonics, I was up and ready for the day. There was, curiously, never a dawn chorus of birdsong, since anything daring to fly in the skies above Calabria would have been shot and eaten. I once opened Luigi's fridge which was bare, barring a dead thrush, de-feathered and destined to add flavour to a tomato sauce.

Every day was active. Before the family trooped up, I would walk down into the valley before the temperature soared, to collect water from the natural spring (there was no piped supply of fresh to the casetta).

The family's livelihood was basic, a self-sufficient *contadini*, or peasant economy, a way of life that, in western Europe, has long disappeared from all but a few remote pockets of the Mediterranean. They grew most of what they ate by cultivating their narrow, stepped terraces by hand. The Devito's livelihood was also supplemented by money sent back from Germany by Domenico.

Although the total land probably amounted to less than half a football pitch, the intensity of production and the range of crops was astounding. There were tomatoes, aubergines, sweetcorn, courgettes, wheat, grapes, cherries, olives, potatoes, figs, hazelnuts, peppers and lemons. And there was the livestock.

Each terrace was irrigated by a clever network of narrow channels which brought water from the higher slopes. Once one terrace had quenched its thirst, the conduit would be dammed by simply moving a clod of earth with a hoe, blocking the stream, while another sluice was opened by removing a second clod.

When it was time to harvest a particular terrace, we would all lend a hand. The wheat required the hardest toil, cut with a small, hand-held sickle, a deft movement which I found highly satisfying once I got the hang of it. This was also the hottest of the tasks but Martina or one of the younger girls from the village would be tasked with keeping the sicklers hydrated. With wine.

The harvesting of the wheat was timed to coincide with the arrival of the 'trebbia', an antiquated, threshing machine that was tractored to a field on the edge of the village. This was a momentous occasion for the locals, its impending arrival rivalled only by the prospect of the Second Coming.

Once sickled, baled and threshed, the sacks of grain were then carried on Martina's or Anna Marie's head, down the footpath and into the village. There they were loaded onto the back seat of my Fiat and driven, with Luigi in the passenger seat, to the miller in the next village. We returned home with the sacks now filled with flour. This became the staple for Anna Marie's tagliatelle, plus loaves of bread, pizzas and biscotti which she baked in an old wood oven that stood in the yard.

In August the village calendar was ignited by two major events: Unita, the communist festival, and the Festa Agosto. It was also the month when scores of migrant workers returned from the production lines of the northern industrial heartlands, streaming down the autostrada in their newish, foreign cars, some with their newish, foreign wives.

Bar talk hummed with tales of construction sites in Zurich, a quarry near the Rhine, a Swiss lift factory, even a plastic bag factory and pints of brown and mild in South Mimms. Domenico also arrived, rather puzzled by my intimate presence in his family, but slowly warming to the situation, writing me off as yet another of his father's more eccentric whims. To celebrate his return, we ate Tonto the turkey (I swear, from his less cocky strutting around the yard during the previous week, he had foretold his own demise).

The seasonal joy was infectious. There were outings to the nearest beach at Copanello, smoky bars full of card players, uniformed musicians playing from a bandstand erected in the piazza, packed churches, firework displays, find-the-lady cardsters, stalls, a carousel, an itinerant Tunisian selling vases covered in shells and, of course, much eating and drinking.

I remember one merry figure, jug of wine in one hand and a salami roll in the other, lifting his arms and telling the world that '*L'Italia e bellissima*', then toppling. From a shawl in the shadows his wife appeared, took the half-eaten roll from his hand, turned to me and said, 'Who would feed our pig if it wasn't for me?' then strode off, leaving her husband to sleep off his excesses where he had toppled.

Festa fever was soon followed by the family's excitement when Estrella gave birth. I was woken by Signor Si, storming into my room in the middle of the night, thrilled to be the first to bring news of the calf's imminent arrival.

Domenico and Luigi were already at work. As soon as two tiny hooves appeared, they tied ropes around the ankles and began heaving. After a lot of hot work and much muscle, and in what then seemed like a mere second, the calf slid out. Estrella turned and licked her baby while Luigi rubbed her down with a towel.

Not long after it was deemed time to take Estrella for slaughtering. She must have sensed something was up and refused to be led out of her room. Luigi, myself and Anna Marie all had to pull hard on a rope attached around her neck. Once we had dragged her out into the daylight she seemed to relax and was easily led along the path, first towards the village, but then branching off the familiar path, climbing high over a saddle and down into the next village of Vallefiorita.

We stopped outside a house and led Estrella, again having to pull hard as if she was aware of mortal danger, down a side alley and into a backyard, open-sided shed where an unfriendly man, in a bloodied T-shirt, shorts and boots, stood under a large hook suspended from a roof beam by chains and pulleys.

After positioning Estrella under the hook, the slaughterer produced a pistol, a stun gun, which he positioned by Estrella's temple and fired, knocking the life out of her. She slumped to the ground and was swiftly hooked and hauled up by her hind legs, inch by inch, to the rafters. The slaughterer then slit her throat.

I won't go through the step-by-step procedures involved in slaughtering. They are gruesome to see and painful to experience. Instead to... job done! I had wondered why Anna Marie had brought four white plastic bags with her, but the answer came just before we set off to walk back to the house. Part of the traditional deal between animal owner and slaughterer, aside from payment for the meat, is that the owner gets to keep most of the offal and that's what was loaded into the bags. We carried it home, all that was left of my old neighbour.

Although the experience was sobering, I never felt there was anything gratuitous about the way Estrella was dispatched. But I did find one incident deeply shocking, one that was to leave a stain on my memory of old Luigi.

One afternoon he found a pine marten caught in a trap, one he'd set earlier for rats. Related to mink and famed for its soft fur, the marten was a handsome creature. Luigi was over the moon at the prospect of being able to sell the pelt for what he imagined would be a small fortune and boasted to everyone about his prize catch. Wearing thick gloves he unclamped it from the trap and put it in an old cage before going to bed.

I was awoken at dawn by the terrifying sounds of animals fighting just outside my window. I got up and stepped outside the *casetta* to see Luigi holding a cast-iron frying pan in the air and chasing after Bruno. Nearby, in a bloodied, mutilated mess on the ground, was the marten. Bruno had clearly managed to open the cage, which must have been poorly secured. Luigi was deranged, screaming abuse at Bruno, whom he eventually collared. With one mighty swing of his arm, Luigi smashed the pan on Bruno's head. The dog collapsed in a heap, stone dead. It was one of the most awful scenes I have ever witnessed and impossible to forget.

I move on.

Whenever you hear the phrase 'the bar scene', it nowadays usually refers to the hottest places in town, serving the grooviest cocktails created by cool mixologists. The bar scene in Amaroni meant something rather different.

There were three bars in the village. One was patronised exclusively by the Communists, the second by the Christian Democrats. A third, which doubled as a small shop, didn't actively promote any ideological allegiance and was run by a lovely man called Laugelli, who always managed to abort any talk of politics by raising his hands in a 'stop the traffic' gesture.

Politics in Amaroni was a matter of passion as well as opinion, the passion verging on aggression, especially so in the run-up to the election of a new village mayor. Virtually every house flew a party flag, red or white, usually attached to the end of a long branch of chestnut or a bamboo pole.

I never witnessed any political violence first hand but half-believed Luigi when he told me that someone's dog had been poisoned and a car's tyres had been slashed. But there was one occasion, when driving back to the village, I encountered a procession of alcohol-infused Communist supporters chanting slogans. I stopped in the road as they approached to let the column pass either side of the car. It was a hot night and my windows were wide open. One young lad, beer bottle in hand, leaned in and warned me that if I killed anyone, I would be killing a Russian!

I also knew of two brothers who married two sisters and both called their first child Raphael after their grandfather, who was still alive and adding to the confusion. But in spite of the apparent strength of the family, political allegiances had cleaved it in two non-speaking factions, so that whenever the brothers passed each other along the street, they refused to even nod good day.

Back to the bars. I made sure that I favoured neither the Communist bar nor the Christian Democrat bar by favouring both in equal measure. Jencarelli, the elder, was invariably seen in the Communist bar, run by a man called Bova whose brother was a lawyer, the top dog in Amaroni and leading contender in the forthcoming election for mayor. Luigi, who was a committed Social Democrat, never drank in either bar but was always particularly put out whenever he saw me having a beer or a coffee with the Communists.

Luigi was not what you'd call a sociable being and probably somewhere on some diagnostic spectrum of autism. It didn't take me long to realise how many of the villagers saw him as a wild card – impulsive, prone to fiery outbursts and irrationality. But that unpredictability was why I was able to be there in the first place. Who but an eccentric old bugger would welcome a stranger from a faraway land so closely into his life?

Back (again) to the bars. Heading back through the village to the *casetta* invariably meant walking a gauntlet of invitations. Bar fly curtains would part, as if disturbed by my passing slipstream, and men would appear, gesturing with thumb and pinky finger tipped up to the mouth in a supping motion.

I mostly made excuses and promised to take up the offer another time. Unfortunately, my apologies only confused matters. The villagers knew I was some sort of writer, so whenever I wanted to politely decline a tipple I would say 'very sorry, but I have to go back to the *casetta* to work'. But for ages I got the verb wrong and told everyone that I needed to go back to '*lavare*', to wash, instead of '*lavorare*', to work.

My best friend in Calabria, someone I liked above all others apart from my surrogate family, was the postman Gino. He didn't live in Amaroni but in nearby Girifalco but came every day with his sackload of deliveries for his allotted round. He and his wife, Maria, also utterly delightful, owned a shack on the beach, one of a row that were built on teetering stilts in the dunes. On Sundays I would often be invited to share a long, lazy lunch.

I would first pick up Gino's young nephew, Marcello, and he and I would go down to the coast early in the morning to fish for octopus. He taught me where to find them, hidden in the rocks, then how to spike them with the trident points on our spear guns and rush them to the surface through a cloud of defensive ink before they had a chance to wriggle off. Once ashore, using thumbs to turn the octopus inside out and expose the muscle in the hub of the body, the one that power-drives the tentacles, you had to pound them on rocks both to kill the animal and tenderise the flesh. Only then would it be ready for the pot or pan.

By the time I had acquired the knack of octopus catching and thumping, I no longer wanted to eat octopus. And I never have since.

Luckily there were other things to eat in Amaroni. Pasta was served in mountainous pyramids at every meal. On Sundays it was always freshly made. Not only was the wheat home-grown, sickled, baled, threshed and ground by the local miller, but the sauce was made from tomatoes raised on the terraces, then chopped, simmered and preserved in recycled beer bottles, each given a leaf of basil before being capped. The pasta would be followed by whatever was ripe or fat enough to eat, perhaps courgettes stuffed with bread, egg and salami, or a piece of beef or chicken. To show my satisfaction, I had to learn a particular gesture, sticking my index finger into the outside of a cheek and rotating it 180 degrees.

The wine, too, was from family grapes. Everyone claimed theirs to be the best, definitely good for you and *'senza medicinae'*, which was meant to imply that you could drink masses of the stuff and never lose your composure or have a hangover. That was so not true.

Because the growing of food was such a core activity in the daily life of rural Calabria, both cooking and consuming were bequeathed immense status. When no longer a stranger in the village, I was frequently invited to eat, not only with my new family but with others. These were special occasions, time for the whitest of tablecloths to be laid, topped by the wedding gift crockery and cutlery.

Aside from eating, and politics, the next most popular topic of conversation was illness, real or imagined. Amaroni was a community of hypochondriacs. Whenever I asked, casually, *'Come stai?'* ('How are you?'), the inevitable response was a long face and a lengthy moan about ailments, invariably to do with the liver (men) or nerves (women).

One time Rocco, the cousin, had to go to hospital. On two or three occasions I took his wife Barbara to visit, each time accompanied by masses of food. I was never sure whether the hospital fed its patients but, even if it did, no self-respecting wife would dream of not providing her husband with her own creations. Nor would she ever doubt that her cooking was superior to anyone else's. Whether there for open heart surgery, a liver transplant, cancer treatment or an amputation, no husband could possibly survive without it. It must have certainly cured Rocco, whom I brought back home after a couple of days. I asked him what had been the problem. 'Liver', he said, although the doctors had found nothing wrong.

One day the priest huffed and puffed his way up to the *casetta* just to see me. I thought he must be bearing bad news, but he came to offer me boiled sweets from his small black briefcase, presumably as an inducement to attend his services. During the recent festival, when the saint's effigy had been paraded through the village, people pinned envelopes of money to her cloak. The priest had later broadcast through the tannoy, positioned high on the church steeple, exactly how much money each donor had contributed. He, along with the doctor and the lawyer Bova, now newly elected as mayor, were the triumvirate of local power. On each of their birthdays they would receive home-made cakes, wine, salamis and other gifts.

The closest of all my relationships was with Little Luigi, Signor Si. We were an odd couple, almost a surrogate father and son during the long absences of his own dad. We went for long walks, he both footpath guide and nature mentor, telling me the names of trees and which berries you could eat. Weirdly, Little Luigi always spoke to me in proper Italian rather than the tricky local dialect, something his family found hilarious.

I took him on his first visit to the sea, even though he'd spent his four years living just a thirty-minute drive away. He was delirious with pleasure, running in and out of the water in ever more daring steps. As soon as he was back in the car for the return drive he fell asleep, was put straight to bed, missed his supper and didn't stir till morning.

One day we planned a long walk. Martina gave us a bag of bread, salami, tomatoes and cheese before we set off. I knew, more or less, where we were going, through the chestnut forests following half-hidden tracks which led up and along the crest of a hill, where we stopped for our picnic. We continued walking. Little Luigi, who had the empty paper bag in his hand, just tossed it into the bushes.

I told him off, explaining as best I could in my feeble Italian, how wrong it was to simply discard rubbish rather than keep it, either until we got back home or passed a bin. Our route took us back through the main street of Amaroni where, just beside the bridge over the occasional, post-rain summertime stream, there was a rubbish bin. I told Little Luigi that this was the place to put his rubbish. My chastisement, the only time I ever appeared cross with him, clearly had soured our otherwise perfect outing, and he went straight to the family's village house rather than walk back to the *casetta* with me.

The next day we were back in full bonding mode, but the incident made me think how, subconsciously, my coming to this remote pocket of Italy would enable me not only to experience a fast-disappearing way of life but that I, the worldly one, could be an enriching influence on the villagers. Explaining to Little Luigi the reckless folly of disrespecting his environment was clearly a case of setting a good example.

One afternoon, soon after my 'lesson', while walking into the village with Little Luigi, we saw the refuse truck. As it approached the bridge, a man jumped out of the cab, walked over to the same rubbish bin and unhooked it from its stand. With the bin in his hand, rather than walk to the back of the truck and empty the contents, he went up to the parapet and tipped the lot straight down onto the dried-up riverbed.

On another occasion, after walking back up the path from the village, I heard screams and yells coming from outside the *casetta*. Big Luigi, Anna Marie and Martina were all shouting at the front door, waving their arms round, putting hands to foreheads or clasping them in prayer. Little Luigi had locked the door with him, and the key, on the inside. Everyone outside was trying to shout instructions at the same time and getting nowhere.

I managed to override the cacophony with a loud '*silencio per favore*' and spoke to Little Luigi, who was understandably very upset at the prospect of the end of the world being proclaimed from the outside. Once calm had been restored it was easy to explain to the lad how to take the key in his hand, hold it tightly between his fingers, and slowly turn it '*a destra*'.

The door opened, Luigi appeared and everyone fell upon him like premier league teammates smothering a goal scorer.

My year in Amaroni came to an end just as spring was blossoming and the circle of life was about to be born again. It wasn't just a question of leaving a place, but separating from a family whose life they'd shared as if I were an adopted son. The parting was tearful. Even Luigi the elder wiped away a tiny droplet from the corner of one eye.

About a year after returning to London, I received a postcard from Martina, the only one of the family able to write. The bulk of the message was devoted to a string of greetings – '*saluti, tanti saluti, ti abbraccio, baci, baci, espero tutti va bene, anche con noi, tutti va bene...*' And then, squeezed into a tiny space at the very bottom of the card, were these words: '*Luigi venire a Londra con il denti Sabato*', which, roughly translated, meant, 'Luigi is to come to London on Saturday with his teeth'.

Some background. Luigi had often complained about his ill-fitting dentures and how it would cost him a small fortune to get them fixed in Calabria. I told him not only that he would be entitled to have a new set in the UK but that I had a really nice dentist friend who would be able to supply them at no cost. I had thought no more about it.

The postcard had arrived on a Friday morning. There was no mention of which Saturday Luigi would be arriving, or how he would be travelling. How could this wiry old trooper, who had only ever left Calabria during a wartime despatch to Ethiopia, manage to reach London? Even leaving the village to go to his nearest big town, Catanzaro, was a rare event. But if ever there was a man cocky enough to take on a challenge, it was Luigi.

I waited in my first-floor North London flat all day Saturday on the off chance he would turn up. On Sunday I went out for a short walk but told my downstairs neighbour about Luigi's possible arrival and asked him to keep an ear open for the doorbell. No Luigi. On Monday I was in the flat for most of the day but decided to see a film in the evening.

I came back around 10.30, opened the front gate, looked through the open curtains into my neighbour's living room and saw Luigi sitting on the sofa. He had been travelling since Saturday, taking a train to Naples, one to Milan, another to Paris. He had managed to take the metro to the Gare du Nord, where he'd caught a train to Calais. He had boarded a ferry and taken another train to London where, at Victoria station, he'd found a taxi and asked the driver to take him to *Davide il Inglese*. Somewhere in his luggage he managed to find a note from Martina with my address.

Against all conceivable odds, Luigi had arrived. An achievement nothing short of miraculous.

Luigi had thought my neighbour, a Canadian roughly the same age as me, was my brother. Why on earth would anyone share the same front door with someone who wasn't family? I led Luigi upstairs to my flat and helped him unpack. He had three items of luggage. One, a large, plastic jerry can filled with his wine. The second, a hold-all full of dried figs stuffed with walnuts by Anna Marie. And the third was a small bag of clothes whose prime function seemed to be to protect half a dozen salamis. How the wine and the food managed to evade the scrutiny of UK customs I never discovered.

My first priority was to schedule, at ludicrously short notice, Luigi's dental appointments. My dentist, John Willis, kindly obliged, first taking the necessary impressions for a complete new set of teeth. Luigi gave him a selection of figs and a salami and told me to decant some of his wine into a bottle, a suitable offering to the great British God of Choppers.

A big question remained. What to do with Luigi during the two weeks he needed to be in London? The fillings, you might say, between the dentistry. Knowing how Luigi's daily life at home revolved entirely around growing things, I decided to put Kew Gardens at the top of the list of outings.

He hated it. In fact, he became really angry at what he saw was a complete waste of land. 'Where are the potatoes?' he protested. 'The tomatoes?'

I did attempt a half-baked explanation as to the importance of horticulture as distinct from agriculture, and why some spaces are more beneficially left green and natural, but he was off, striding away to inspect, in further disbelief, Kew's pagoda.

He then became besotted by the sky and the sight of low-flying aircraft on their final approaches to nearby Heathrow. I decided to cut short the tour of the gardens and head for the airport.

In those days you could park on the open top deck of the multi-storey car park and survey the entire airfield and the frequent comings and goings, with nothing to obscure the view. As soon as I'd parked, Luigi leapt from the car and ran straight to the barrier with an expression of pure wonderment. It reminded me of the look on his grandson's face when he saw the sea for the very first time.

From the car park we walked into the arrivals hall, where the next thing to stop Luigi in his tracks was a large group of Hasidic Jews who were clearly there to meet and greet someone very important. Luigi went up close, almost mingling with the befrocked, bearded and behatted men, staring without reservation. He then turned to me and loudly proclaimed how they were all '*monci*', meaning monks, but a word that could have been seriously misconstrued. Luckily the customs hall door opened at that moment and the figure of a Hasidic elder came through, and the meeters and greeters roared with excitement, jumping up and down and clapping and hugging and forgetting all about the slight and shrivelled figure of an offensive Luigi.

Sunday was earmarked for a roast with my parents, who lived in the tower block of a council estate near Warren Street. My dad was particularly excited. I had told him all about Luigi's wine and I had also told Luigi about my dad's vintage.

For his last birthday I had bought him a home wine-making kit, the essential ingredients being a can of some sort of grape juice, various glass tubes and rubber stoppers, and a set of Bacchanalian sticky labels where the name of the wine and the viticulturalist could be added in a space framed by drawings of bunches of grapes and cherubic quaffers.

Lunch was served. My dad made a bit of a show of opening a bottle of Chateau Wickers claret before pouring a taster into Luigi's glass. Like a professional sommelier, he stepped back to await his approval.

Luigi took one sip and spat it out, all over the Sunday best tablecloth. '*Questo non e vino*,' he declared, then apologised for the mess and started to mop it up with his napkin. At first my dad was clearly upset but he then began to feel sorry for this noble savage whom his son had imported, someone who had thoughtfully given my mum a salami sausage and some stuffed figs.

Another day, another outing, this time to South Mimms, where Salvatore, my day-one Amaroni translator, had lived. We went to visit some of his relatives whom I'd previously met in Amaroni during the August festival. The house, from the front, was a quintessential English, suburban semi, white with black mock Tudor beams. In the back, the differences could not have been more dramatic. The entire garden was completely devoted to vegetables, the potting shed home to a grape press and huge vats.

Luigi didn't seem too happy with the visit. It was all rather formal, the family's living room furnished with chairs that lined the walls like a waiting room. We left when we politely could. That evening, to lighten the mood, I took Luigi to see *Amarcord*, a mad, comic, anarchic Fellini fantasy in which one of the women characters lifts her blouse to reveal her boobs to a teenage lad. The scene induced such a loud, explosive guffaw from Luigi that the upper plate of his old dentures broke from their mooring on the roof of his mouth and dropped into his lap.

After ten days, the new set of teeth was ready and Luigi returned for his final fitting. John Willis offered him a hand mirror and Luigi was well pleased with his new, Mentos-white smile. The next day I double-checked his return ticket and took him to Victoria to catch the Dover train. I felt sad to see him go but, I admit, immensely relieved.

I only once returned to Amaroni, some three years after Luigi's visit. I flew into Calabria's brand-new airport, Lamezia Terme, picked up a car, drove to the village, parked in the piazza and walked up the main street. As if time had stood still, familiar men emerged from the fly-screened bars offering me a glass of wine and said they knew that when Luigi had been in London I'd taken him to see a bare-breasted woman!

I picked up the familiar footpath that led from the road up to the terraced hillsides. Whenever Anna Marie or Martina used to approach the *casetta*, on occasions when the Luigis had spent the night there, they would cry out a piercing 'Ah, Luigi' as they walked the final stretch of the path. On this occasion I did the same, as loud and as shrilly as I could manage.

A few seconds later, while still some thirty or forty yards from the *casetta*, I heard screams. Anna Marie and Martina appeared and came hurtling down the path towards me, yelling my name over and over and enveloping me in hugs and kisses. No words were spoken until the initial passion had subsided and we turned to continue up the path where, at the top, Luigi stood coolly leaning against his hoe. Anna Marie suddenly stopped in her tracks, turned towards me and asked if I'd eaten.

I was only there for the day. I stayed until Little Luigi, no longer so little, returned from school. He stood rooted to the spot when he saw me, then ran up for a hug that never seemed to end.

Amaroni is now only a memory. Most of the village elders, including Anna Marie and Luigi, will have passed away. Martina and Domenico will be as ancient as I am, while Little

Luigi and Anna Marie will no doubt have their own families. Franco has died and I no longer have contact with my Swiss friends. But, writing these words has made me want to travel back, in both time and place.

7

OFF PISTE

One winter weekend, while I was living just outside the Swiss lakeside town of Lucerne, my friend Franco suggested that we, along with a group of friends, should spend Sunday on the nearest ski slopes. I said it sounded like fun and I'd be delighted to join everyone but, as I had never skied before, I'd probably go walking instead and meet up with everyone later. Franco said he'd bring a spare pair of skis, sticks and boots, just in case I fancied having a go.

Franco worked for Rossignol, the local ski company, which made skis worn by Olympic champions. I've always believed, when it comes to any sporting activity, that complete beginners should never economise on equipment. They need all the help they can get. So I wasn't intimidated by the idea of using Rossignol skis and felt confident that, after a quick lesson, I'd be at least able to progress to the nursery slopes by lunchtime and even tackle a blue or a red run by the end of the afternoon. Bring it on…

I didn't, however, put the theory into practice as far as clothing went. I had not yet bought any proper outdoor gear, let alone fancy ski wear. On Sunday I set off to meet everyone wearing jeans, a thick sweater and a belted Burberry raincoat.

We drove the snaking road up to one of the ski resorts on the Rigi mountain. We parked and walked up a gentle slope to a place, close to the ski lift, where absolute beginners could have a basic introductory lesson or two before committing to a proper slope. The plan was for Franco to help me to don boots and skis while the others took the lift to the top station and hurtle down the serious runs.

I undid the belt on my raincoat, put on the boots and skis, with Franco's help, and looked down the slope. Just as Franco began to tell me how to snow plough to a stop, my skis decided they didn't need any lessons and started to take off. I stood rigidly upright, tried in vain to spike the poles into the snow to stop – a dangerous manoeuvre, according to skiers – and slowly gathered momentum. I headed straight for the line of people queuing for the lift.

I must have looked like a Looney Tunes cartoon figure, raincoat billowing behind like a pair of broken wings, a grin verging on a grimace spreading across my face. My speed gradually increased. As the people in the line looked up and saw me approach, they first slowly parted, then leapt out of the way. I managed to sail through a gap, still smiling like a complete idiot. There were a couple of yelps and even a scream as I sliced through the crowd, but the only proper words I heard came from a man who exclaimed, 'But, he's wearing Rossignol.' Moments later, I came to a spectacular fall, completely unharmed except for severely damaged pride.

8

BIG MARY

We – my wife Charlotte and our six-month-old daughter Francesca – flew to Ireland, into Kerry, and took a taxi from the airport to Tralee. I gave the driver the address of the stables where we had booked a horse and gypsy caravan for the weekend. 'Now, tell me,' the driver pondered, 'why would a couple of big city folk like yourselves, not to mention your little baby there, be wanting to spend a weekend peering up the backside of a horse?'

Good question. I was about to explain how we really fancied a few days savouring life in the slow lane, but thought that, maybe, he could take offence at the suggestion of 'slow'. I had been told that Kerry folk were often at the butt end of such Irish jokes as: 'What do they stamp on the bottom of bottles of Guinness distributed in Kerry?' Answer: 'Open other end'. I just said how we fancied getting away from London and seeing some lovely countryside.

The backside we were soon to face belonged to Big Mary,

the horse we had been allocated by the Tralee stable manager. It was, in fact, discreetly veiled by a thick tail, though not soundproofed, her idle stomach trumpetings resonating like a German brass section warming up for an oompah concert.

Big Mary loomed as big as a double-decker. I felt like muttering a rather wimpish, 'We did have something a little smaller in mind,' while tentatively stroking her nose, but Joe, the chief horse hand, assured us that Big Mary was quiet and even-tempered. Later we wondered whether he'd said 'quite' even-tempered.

Until then, my closest ever encounter with a horse had been astride a donkey on the sands of Great Yarmouth when I was six. But the brochure did promise: 'If you have little or no experience of horses, have no worries. All our horses have plenty of experience with people.' Well, that's OK then.

Our caravan, made of wood and modelled on traditional Romany lines, was crimson with yellow 'go faster' stripes and a bitumen-black humped back. For 'Romany' also read basic. The cramped interior contained a small double bed, a two-ring gas burner, a sink that emptied straight onto the road through a rude dangle of hosepipe, plenty of pots, pans and plates but no fridge or toilet. We kept the milk and baby's food cool in the oats box attached to the back of the caravan and Ireland's bushy hedgerows were to prove a blessing for comfort stops.

We were shown how to harness, groom, feed and water Big Mary. We were also handed an owner's manual with 'dos and don'ts', the last do telling us to 'return the caravan to base after use'.

The parting words from the stable manager were cautionary. 'Remember, Big Mary knows her way around but will always take the shortest route without allowing for the width of the caravan.' We later spied streaks of crimson and yellow livery warpaint on the grey parapet of a granite bridge. We also met a Dane in clogs with a cut on his nose. He had gone and done a 'don't', namely to let go of the reins. His horse had romped off in search of greener grass while still tethered to the caravan. The wheels had sunk into a ditch and the Dane came tumbling after.

We set off. The driving seat at the front of the caravan, a narrow wooden platform no wider than a bookcase shelf, turned out to be less precarious than it first appeared, but you had to be careful not to get your legs caught in the turning shaft. Or, indeed, by Big Mary when she ceremoniously raised her tail.

Everything appeared straightforward. For the first five minutes. Then Big Mary decided to stop for no good reason in the middle of the Tralee traffic. Amazingly, a few cries of 'giddy up' did the trick and, empowered by our newly discovered horsemanship, we confidently rode on.

We delved into the glorious Dingle peninsula, the hedgerows alive with wild fuchsias and montbretia, with the green of Kerrygold dairy meadows beyond. We clip-clopped steadily along while every joint in the caravan creaked like an ancient galleon.

For all her height and mightiness, Big Mary was, of course, only one horsepower, half the thrust of a Citroen 2CV. So she, we, only travelled at walking pace, enabling us to take turns on the reins while the other strolled alongside. At one point I even got off to buy a bar of chocolate and was still able to canter up and climb back on board the moving caravan with Charlotte on the driver's plank.

On the first night we camped at a village called Camp. We steered the caravan into a half circle of others, just like a John Ford western, on a patch of green behind a pub. We unharnessed the rig, laid the shafts to rest on the grass and led Big Mary to her meadow for the night (another do from the manual: 'Close gates or your horse will make its own way back to base').

The pub had good food and facilities, plus live music and a peat fire. Bliss. We all slept well. The next morning began with a ritual called 'first catch your horse'. There's a knack, as detailed in the dos. You put some tasty oats, full of goodness, into a bucket and walk into the fields reciting a stream of Hail Marys. What the dos didn't explain was how to hold your ground when every other grazing horse comes trotting over, knowing just what you've got in the bucket. I now know how a lone infantryman must have felt facing the charge of the Light Brigade.

Harnessing proved a harder task than untethering. We stared hopelessly at the tagliatelle of leather, of hames and housen, trace strap and breeching strap, laid out on the ground, while Big Mary stared in the other direction. I could swear I heard her whistling impatiently.

We gave in and asked the pub's barman, who was clearing out last night's empties, to lend a hand, fearful that if we got things wrong, a breezy giddy-up would send Big Mary sliding straight off the ends of the cart shafts with a 'hey nonny nonny and an oats to you'. According to last night's horse talk around the bar, that's exactly what happened to four German lads from Wiesbaden who had to hire a taxi for a 'follow that horse' pursuit.

One horsepower sets an upper limit of about twelve miles a day, so you can't travel far in a weekend. On day two we dipped further into the Dingle peninsula, following the coastal plain along the north shore. We spent the second night at Sandy Bay, a flat sandy spit with a spine of marram-capped dunes. The next day, as the rest of the British Isles basked in a cloudless scorcher, it rained. Torrential outbursts soaked both Big Mary and whoever sat on the plank while the other two steamed in the caravan. Smoky clouds hid almost everything above chimney pot level.

But what's a drop of rain? 'Envy those colourful travellers,' read a tourist board promotion, 'roaming the rainbows of Ireland, laden with nothing but freedom, always travelling but forever home.' I didn't see a single rainbow.

We returned to base with no mishaps other than having to hold back Big Mary who, sensing home and a nice snug stable, suddenly opened her throttle in the middle of Tralee. I had to use every ounce of muscle to stop her rounding the corner by the bridge and adding to those coloured stripes. Perhaps that's what they meant by the rainbows of Ireland.

9

THE BOOK THAT NEVER WAS

After writing a school textbook on *Commercial Life* for the (now-defunct) publisher Harrap, my editor commissioned me to write a book on white-collar crime. Although I barely knew anything about the subject, I was both excited and flattered to be asked, so immediately agreed.

Within just a few days of my initial research, I was completely hooked. It not only seemed to be a subject that tapped a deep, political seam but, best news of all, there was no other book on the subject.

In essence, white-collar crimes are the ones we rarely hear about. Despite causing enormous financial suffering, social harm and occasional physical injury, even death, their mostly middle-class, respectable perpetrators – whether individuals or corporations – are seldom treated with anything like the severity metered out to the typical crimes committed by lower-class crooks. By comparison, white-collar criminals are rarely arrested or prosecuted, let alone incarcerated, despite the damaging consequences of their actions which dwarf most traditional crimes. The more I looked into the subject, the more engrossed I became and the more outrage I felt at the injustices encompassed by the very name.

This is not the place to delve further into the essence of white-collar crime, but I would just like to include a verse from an anonymous folk poem that somehow best summarises the subject matter.

> The law locks up the man or woman
> Who steals the goose from off the common
> But let's the greater felon loose
> Who steals the common from the goose.

Or one attributed to Anatole France:

> 'The law, in its majestic equality, forbids the rich as well as the poor to sleep under bridges, to beg in the streets, and to steal bread.'

Although my advance from Harrap was slim, I managed to find work as a part-time lecturer at an art school, which covered my every day, modest living expenses. In the UK, I divided my time between the British Library, then housed in the magnificent 19th Reading Room* inspired by the domed Panthenon in Rome**, and the Institute of Criminology at Cambridge. Since many of the most flagrant abuses of power took place in the USA, I also spent time researching cases in New York, where I met the incredibly helpful (and recently deceased) Robert Morgenthau, the District Attorney for Manhattan.

The book took around eighteen months to write. As it neared completion, I managed, after weeks of trying, to set up an interview with Commander Crane, who was head of the UK's Fraud Squad. The experience, especially for a twenty-seven-year-old, was hugely intimidating and very different from the time I had spent with Morgenthau.

I was met in the foyer at Scotland Yard by a public relations exec who escorted me to Crane's office. As we squeezed into the lift, sandwiched between burly, plain-clothes coppers, he told what an amazing job the commander was doing in investigating several serious fraud cases, one of the most common brands of white-collar crime.

Commander Crane, immaculately dressed in a light grey suit, shook my hand and told the PR man to sit to one side and take notes. I sat in front of Crane's enormous desk, bare except for three items: a completely unmarked, leather-framed blotting pad; a large crystal ball set on a plinth; and a copy of Erich von Daniken's *Chariot of the Gods*, turned so that the cover and title were facing me.

The book, for those who have not come across it, advances the theory that earth was once visited by extra-terrestrial aliens who, as evidence of their presence, had left behind various artefacts and inexplicable markings on the land. The most famous of the latter are the Nazca lines, discovered in a remote desert in Peru and supposedly created as navigational aids for visiting space craft. Published in the late sixties, the book achieved something of a cult status among a young, impressionable demographic.

Now, here's the first uncool thing I did. Rather than ignoring what was, in hindsight, clearly intended to produce a reaction, I prattled on about how the book was really interesting, thereby painting myself into a loosely defined 'alternative' corner.

From then on, Commander Crane made complete mincemeat of my embryonic skills as an investigative journalist. When I first stepped into his office, I was poised to fire a number of questions covering several white-collar crimes and misdemeanours that the Fraud Squad had seemingly failed to investigate. But Crane simply beat me to it, pre-empting my questions by citing the very same cases as examples of what he and his team were doing to apprehend those responsible.***

I was utterly humiliated. I had barely got my breath back, let alone picked up my sword, before Crane indicated that my allotted time was up, asked the PR man to escort me out, sat down at his desk, picked up the *Chariot of the Gods* and slipped it into his drawer.

Despite the setback, I finished the book soon after and handed it to my editor. It was well received and Harrap devoted a full page to it in their 'Forthcoming Publications' booklet. I was riding on a cloud.

It didn't take long for the cloud to burst. A few days after the pre-publication promotion, the editor telephoned to ask if I was able to meet. I said of course, when would that be? This week sometime?

No, he said. He needed to see me 'right now'. Urgently.

Very odd. I arrived at Harrap's in just over an hour after the call. The editor, who shared the office with his PA, immediately ushered her out of the room and closed the door. 'There's bad news', he said. 'Special Branch called earlier this morning and told me they had a file on you.'

On me? Whatever for? I had never been arrested, let alone convicted of any crime, white-collar or otherwise. If Special Branch had a file on me, I pointed out, they would have one on half the population in Britain, including the editor. And probably his PA.

'But,' he continued, 'they had so much detail. They knew your father was a civil servant.' True, but he was a low-grade clerical officer in the Ministry of Supply. And had never even voted Labour, let alone plotted a Guy Fawkes act of rebellion or bonded with the likes of Philby, Blunt or Burgess.

'They were also aware that you'd been to Czechoslovakia.'

Yes, on a holiday with a girlfriend. Again, she was no anarchist but an aspiring fashion model. She grew up in

Bromley, for Pete's sake. Her father worked for Esso and her mother, whenever there was a guest in the house, used to put toilet rolls into brown paper bags before carrying them from her shopping bag to the upstairs loo.

'Ah, but they said you were going to live in Czechoslovakia.' Again, yes… and no. The British Council had awarded me a scholarship to study at the FAM film school in Prague, but I had turned it down (long story, but nothing remotely to do with espionage).

They also said they had evidence that in 1968, I was at the anti-Vietnam war demo in front of the American Embassy on Grosvenor Square, one that had turned fairly violent. True, but how would they know? There were hundreds of people there. The scary part was not that they had anything of any significance on me, but that they even had a file in the first place.

The editor saved the clincher until the end of the meeting. Special Branch had suggested to Harrap that their intention to publish *White Collar Crime* was, perhaps, not in the publisher's best interest. The editor also added that, despite personally coming from the 'publish and be damned' school, he felt it necessary to raise the matter with one of his directors, who decided that it would be unwise for the company to antagonise the police in case they imposed an injunction on the book's publication.

It had taken just a short call, probably from one of Commander Crane's minions, to convince a leading publisher so dramatically to change gear from being super-enthusiastic about the book to deciding to abort the entire project.

In short, Harrap threw in the towel, with gushing apologies, and I rode the tube back home with my fat, multi-page manuscript in the PA's spare Sainsbury's carrier bag.

I was both emotionally flattened and fearful. On the tube, I looked nervously at the other passengers, thinking one of them could be tailing me, maybe with a view to grabbing the bag.

For several days I was convinced my phone was being tapped. But then fear turned into anger and I was determined to find another publisher.

I first approached a company that had shown interest in another book proposal, one I had submitted a few weeks prior to my starting work on *White Collar Crime*. The new publisher was much more cavalier and, when I told him about the book's recent history, refused to be intimidated by Special Branch. Having been involved in South Africa's anti-apartheid movement, his political background rather piqued his interest in challenging the authorities, rather than being deterred by any veiled threat.

However, rather than give me an advance on publication, he felt he needed the money to commission a specialist libel lawyer to read the manuscript. Although I convinced him that every single fact I had included had already been in the public domain, he wanted to be reassured there was nothing too contentious in the content that might lead to one of the companies or individuals mentioned issuing a writ.

The lawyer was not happy. Such is the intrinsic nature of white-collar crime that many of the cases highlighted in the book, all indisputably having inflicted financial, social and physical harm, had not yet led to prosecutions or convictions in a court of law. He argued that to use the word 'crime' in the title of a book could justify claims from those named individuals or corporations that they were defamed or libelled merely by being included in the first place.

Publisher number two, while bravely willing to fight a political battle was, not unreasonably, unwilling to risk being sued. Time, therefore, for a second ride home on the tube, manuscript in a bag (I'd taken my own bag with me this time), but at least I no longer felt I was under surveillance.

So, back to nowhere. That is, until I got a call from publisher number three. He had been contacted by my Harrap editor, who was still convinced that *White Collar Crime* ought to see the light of day (especially as the book was his idea in the first place). The third company was a small, independent, Marxist-leaning imprint. My new editor promised he had no problem being targeted by the wrath of the establishment if it meant *White Collar Crime* made waves. Big ones.

Since publisher number three had a reputation for books that were rooted in a far more academic contexts than mine, the editor asked how I felt about involving a well-known sociologist to work on the manuscript and, ultimately, help to create a book that had more gravitas. I happily agreed. Anything to get the book out there.

The new enemy was neither Special Branch nor libel lawyers, but time. It had now been over a year since I delivered the manuscript to Harrap. The sociologist also needed to complete a project he was currently working on before getting stuck into *White Collar Crime*. The editor raised an obvious question, one that I had been aware of, but didn't really want to confront.

Most of case studies that I had used in creating the original book were rapidly becoming outdated. At the same time, a number of new ones would not be covered unless, basically, I did an enormous amount of work, a task that would need many weeks, if not months, with no financial backing. Publisher number three worked on a shoestring. I had to earn a living.

I am writing this tale over forty years later. Roughly ten feet to the left of where I am now sitting, perched on a shelf gathering dust, is a large box file marked *White Collar Crime*.

It is the book that never was.

NOTES

* The layout of the Reading Room was based on a hub and spoke design, the hub being where the librarians were based, with long wooden desks reaching along the

several spokes. One day, at the time when the IRA were threatening to blow up buildings in London, one of the librarians stood up to address a section of desks on the side of the room opposite to where I was sitting. After his brief words, everyone in that section stood up and walked out of the building. Such were the acoustics that I could not make out a single word, just a staccato of echoing sounds.

The librarian then addressed a second section to my left, but again neither I, nor anyone sitting near me, could make out a single word. Again, everyone within earshot also stood and abruptly left the building. Finally, the librarian turned towards my seating area. 'We have just been informed by the police,' he said with total clarity, 'that there has been a bomb threat targeting the museum, so could everyone please leave the building.'

** Despite the silence in the main Reading Room, there was an area reserved for those wanting to use typewriters. With room for around a dozen, it was a very sociable place and I made new friends. Knowing that I was planning a trip to South America, one of them gave me the name of his friends who worked for the British Council in Lima. I spent a few happy days in their company before they, in turn, arranged for me to stay with their friends in a small village on the shores of Lake Titicaca. He was a Jesuit missionary. He looked like Steve McQueen, smoked cigars, made knockout Pisco sours and was living with an English nurse.

*** Commander Crane, soon after my interview, went on to collar John Poulson, who was convicted in 1973 for one of the biggest corruption/bribery scandals, one which also brought down Sir Reginald Maudling, then Home Secretary. Crane was later knighted. I had also covered the Poulson story in my book, prior to his conviction.

10

SANTA LIVES

Our check-in line at Gatwick was easy to spot. It was the one with the elf. On the flight to Rovaniemi in far north Finland there was tinsel hanging from the ceiling, 'God Rest Ye Merry Gentlemen' feeding through the PA and a fairy with wings, tiara and a tutu did the safety drill. A steward wore a big red nose (a false one, not the result of testing the duty-frees).

Someone, somewhere, has calculated that on Christmas Eve, Father Christmas would have to cover more than 100 million miles, travelling at 1,000 miles per second, in order to make all his promised deliveries. Now, either that means the Santa thingy is a complete load of tosh or it's a complete load of magic. Personally we favour the latter. And that's because the 'we' in question – me and my (then) seven-year-old son Jonah – went to see him. The real one, that is, at his home in Finnish Lapland, not some department store sales assistant dressing up for the silly season.

Although it has rather cornered the market in Father Christmas pilgrimages, Finland has not gone quite as far as a New York department store that once advertised 'Six Santas. No Waiting'.

At Rovaniemi airport, the control tower was festooned with fairy lights and crowned by a giant red neon star. It was 1.30pm but already beginning to get dark. Or not beginning to get light. Although more famous in summer as the land of the midnight sun, Lapland in winter is the land of the midday dark. And cold. Minus twelve degrees! Not a twelve degree Fahrenheit nip in the air but a bone-chilling minus twelve Celsius. Who'd be a Finn, I thought. Who'd be Santa?

We boarded a coach, nice and snug, and drove into the black and white night, the headlights revealing trees upon trees rising from a thick duvet of snow. We were told that there could well be elves along the road but we didn't spot any. My son was disappointed but I wasn't surprised. If they had any sense, all elves would be tucked up indoors, watching the telly.

Our roost was the family-run Harriniva, a 'wilderness holiday centre' on the banks of the river Muonionjoki, which we couldn't really see because it just looked like more snow. Sweden, we were told, lay on the opposite shore. The lodge, like a super-size-me log cabin, was originally built for German adventurers as a stopover en-route to the North Pole. On the inside, it looked like the innards of a sauna, fully pine-clad and with more layers of insulation than a pass-the-parcel package.

We checked into our room, which had a log fire and even a private sauna. The wardrobe had already been stocked with Ranulph Fiennes-wear: outer thermal onesies, moon boots, gloves and top mittens and thick tea cosy top-hats to be worn on top of Johnny English balaclavas.

We had dinner, of soup ('better than London soup', according to Jonah), followed by salmon pinned on board and roasted on an open fire, then tucked up for the night like a couple of well-honeyed bears. It was all so cosy and comforting that I half thought we might spend the next couple of days without bothering to venture into the wickedly cold world beyond, where even breath from a whisper rose like a steam train.

But of course, the next morning, after first layering up so that only our eyes were left to chance the elements, we did step outside. For the next few days I greeted everyone we passed like an old friend, just in case we'd previously chatted 'undressed' in the lounge or dining room.

Grown-ups should really turn the 'visit Santa experience' on its head and think not just about an audience with the bearded one, with a few snowy distractions on the side, but a menu of soft adventures in the snow, with Santa as a celebrity bonus.

We rode, swaddled beneath deer skins, on a sleigh pulled by a reindeer which I passed off as Rudolph, explaining how his nose only shines for night flights (a little-known Finnish Aviation Authority regulation).

We visited the husky kennels, where forty barking, growling, howling but incredibly friendly and cuddly hounds were desperate for some action. Six were tied to our sled and I stood at the back on what looked like a zimmer frame, feet firmly on the brake, its steel claws bedded into the snow but only just able to hold back the hounds, who were desperate for the take-off. We then mush mushed off, a timeless ride through a silent world of a zillion conifers, everywhere insulated by thick snow. That evening we enjoyed the ultimate boys' toy, a snowmobile, my boy yelling, 'Faster, faster,' from the pillion as we roared along on the crust of the frozen river.

Next day we went to a reindeer farm where we sat around a fire, inside a traditional Sami tepee, cooking sausages and drinking warm rose hip tea in the company of a charismatic old shaman dressed in furs, before taking a sleigh ride pulled by reindeers. We were offered the chance of a swim in an ice hole but we said, 'No thanks, some other time, perhaps.'

Of course we were hoping to see the Northern Lights but had been warned that they could well be hidden by cloud, or just fail to turn up like petulant rock stars. But one night, after supper, Jonah and I took a walk from the lodge and climbed a hill. Nothing special in that... or so we thought. At the summit the lights, THE lights, suddenly appeared, decorating the night sky with a show of brilliant greens. We oohed and aahed. It was like seeing the wind at work, wispy tendrils flexing, weaving and waving in a magical, other-worldy choreography.

Santa was, of course, the star turn. Dad and son were swaddled in elk skins in a sled and pulled into the heart of darkness by a flying Finn on a snowmobile. Ice sparkled in the pines like fireflies, snowy meadows radiated a ghostly blue light. Even fully bundled up against the cold, I felt a real, scary sense of the wild Arctic, icy fangs of death licking across the valley floor.

For the last half mile, the track through the forest was lined with flaming torches. We saw a lonely cabin, a des-res in the absolute middle of nowhere, lights radiating from within like an advent calendar. An elf greeted us at the door and escorted us into Santa's home, a glowing womb of good tidings, a scene so exceedingly perfect. A pair of elves were busy wrapping presents to the side while the man himself sat on a big throne.

I was half dreading the encounter, imagining all sorts of naff jollity, with give-away glimpses of Hush Puppies and M&S ankle socks peeking from the bottom of the red robe. But here was a real pro, with a beard big and bushy enough to hide a flock of starlings. He wore little round specs, big red boots, and had rouged cheeks. Instead of dispensing the usual 'ho ho ho, been a good boy?' patter, Santa spoke about the spirit of Christmas and how he was prepping for the big eve ahead. I was impressed and so was the boy who, for a rare moment in his waking life, was reduced to silent gawping. When he shook hands I thought Jonah was about to teeter over backwards like a Coldstream guard during a Trooping the Colour heatwave.

Santa also turned up at supper on the last night. He pulled up in his reindeered sleigh and all the children charged across the dining room. Had we been a ship we would have instantly capsized. He staggered in with the help of a cane, sat encircled by kids and opened his sack, giving each individual child exactly what they had written to ask for. Now there's magic for you.

If you don't want to spoil things, shut your eyes now. I had brought Jonah's present in a suitcase, hidden in a black bin liner, and sneaked it to the receptionist on arrival. And Santa? Not telling.

11

SCENT OF A DOG

We used to have a dog, a Golden Retriever called Boysie. Bought from a breeder, he was one of a litter of five. When we went to pick him up from the kennels, we learned that Nicole Farhi had already chosen one of his siblings. It was reassuring to know that we shared the designer's impeccable taste.

Fast forward by five or six years, to Nice on the Cote d'Azur. I was there to write a travel feature on the city, with a focus on some of the artists who made it their home. Among the places I wanted to visit was the Matisse museum in the suburb of Cimiez. I also wanted to see a building nearby where Matisse once lived and which, I was told by a guide, had a magnificent main staircase and colonnaded foyer.

The *belle epoque* building, the Regina Palace, was built in the late nineteenth century as a hotel for British aristocrats, including Queen Victoria, who often overwintered in Nice. It was later converted into a number of elegant apartments.

When I arrived, however, I discovered that, before I could even get close to the main entrance, there was an outer gate secured by an entry code.

I did consider ringing a few of the brass bells on a panel beside the residents' names, on the off chance that someone would simply buzz me in without asking for any ID, but decided the place was rather too grand for such feral behaviour.

Just as I was about to abort the mission, a man arrived at the gate and asked, in perfect English, if he could help. When I explained what I was doing in Nice, and how I'd hoped to see the foyer, he – a resident – kindly invited me to take a look. The entrance hall and staircase were every bit as impressive as I'd been told.

I asked on which floor Matisse had lived. 'The fourth,' the man replied. 'As a matter of fact, I live in the apartment next door. If you like, you're welcome to come and have a look because I share exactly the same view that he famously painted.'

Amazing. I thanked him, several times, as we rode up in the lift and stepped into his elegant apartment. Several original paintings and limited-edition prints were displayed on the walls, none by Matisse, but I did spot a drawing by Picasso. He – Paul – showed me the 'Matisse view' through the window.

I felt it wise not look around too inquisitively, just in case he suspected my story to be an elaborate ploy to case the joint, prior to returning to nick its treasures. Aside from his collection of artworks, my eye did take in a number of family photos, including one of a Golden Retriever. 'Oh, I've just seen your dog,' I remarked. 'He's almost identical to my own Golden Retriever.'

'Really?' he replied. 'They are a lovely, affectionate breed. She's not mine, though. She belongs to my sister. She's rather famous in England, so you probably have heard of her. Nicole Farhi?'

I explained what seemed to me to be an extraordinary coincidence. Paul agreed and kindly gave me his sister's email address. She also lived in North London, close to our own house.

When I got home, I sent Nicole Farhi an email, explaining what had happened and suggesting that our pooches might like to meet up for a 'family' walk on Hampstead Heath. I never did receive a reply, which I'm afraid makes a rather feeble end to this little tale. But at least Boysie didn't feel my sense of rejection.

12

PISTE OFF

When my daughter Maddy was nine years old, she broke her leg skiing. She had never skied before. The accident happened within the first thirty minutes, on her very first day, on the nursery slopes.

We were staying in the oddly named but beautifully located village of Hogfjells, in the middle of the Norwegian nowhere. Maddy was having a private lesson, sharing a highly experienced senior instructor with her twelve-year-old sister. While easing down a nursery slope, her skis parted, her legs splayed in two different directions, her ankle twisted and her tibia snapped just above the rim of the boot.

We took a taxi from the slopes to a doctor in the nearest town. The GP practice had its own X-ray machine, which seemed both reassuring and indicative of what must be a frequent occurrence in a ski resort. After checking the image, the doctor declared that Maddy had 'a classic fracture'. Another taxi was summoned. Maddy's leg was encased in an inflatable splint and we were driven some distance to the hospital at Lillehammer in the heart of Norway's ski country.

The taxi driver said she would happily wait and take us back to Hogfjells after the operation. At the entrance to A&E they wheeled Maddy in on a trolley and parked her in a corridor immediately beneath a poster of the 1994 Winter Olympics, staged in Lillehammer. I completed the hospital paperwork.

If you are going to break a leg, Lillehammer is a good place to do it. The hospital repairs more snapped limbs than any other procedure. The staff, who all spoke near-perfect English, were very sensitive and reassuring to a terrified little girl. They always first introduced themselves to Maddy, asking her all the necessary questions, before turning to me for confirmation or clarification.

Things happened seamlessly but slowly. We played a lifetime's worth of Hangman. Our Hangman also only ever had one leg. After a second batch of X-rays we waited another couple of hours for a slot in the theatre schedule.

We had hoped to return to Hogfjells, and Maddy's mother, sister and brother, the same evening, but we were told that Maddy would need to stay overnight. A nurse showed us into a children's ward where they had set up a bed for me, next to Maddy's, and produced towels and toothbrushes. We left our winter clothing in the bedside locker and waited to be summoned to the theatre.

My daughter needed a general anaesthetic, administered by a German called Jurgen who was very proud of his new calculator which allowed him to convert Madeleine's weight in stones and pounds into kilos (I know, old hat these days but state of the art back in the day). At around nine o'clock in the evening, a porter came to take us to the theatre where they robed me in a green, backless number, a plastic mop cap and a pair of clogs of a design I last wore in the sixties. I warned the surgeon he might have two snapped tibias to deal with if I had to hobble any distance.

They let me stay with Maddy right up to the moment the anaesthetic took over before swiftly ushering me away. I was told I could wait in the recovery room, where Maddy would arrive some thirty minutes later, at around midnight. Outside the theatre I de-robed and unclogged, dressed, ambled along a corridor, found the recovery room and was about to see if there was somewhere to get a coffee and a sandwich when I suddenly remembered our taxi driver.

Rather than go all the way back to the ward to collect my warm outdoor clothing, and wearing just a T-shirt, jeans and trainers, I followed an exit sign, hurried outside, quickly found the driver, who was contentedly knitting and listening to the radio in her Volvo, and explained the situation. She was not in the least bit put out. I signed her fare sheet which, including waiting time, was around £200 (more like £400 or £500 at today's prices), the bill then going straight to the hospital.

I thanked her, said goodbye and turned back to the door from where I had just exited, but I could not get back inside. Presumably, for security reasons, the door only opened outwards. I waited to see if anyone came out but, in the middle of the night, there was no sign of anyone.

I don't recall the temperature that night but it was well below freezing. I rapidly began to chill. Needing urgently to find the main entrance, or perish from hypothermia, I began to jog, all round the outside of the huge hospital complex. I got hopelessly lost. On the far side of car park, I saw the lone figure of a woman. I ran up to her. She turned, rather startled, to see this mad, underdressed, non-Norwegian speaking, and obviously panicking, person pleading for a 'way in'.

Had this occurred in the USA, she would probably have shot me. But, being Norwegian, she kindly, in English, pointed the way to the main entrance. I ran through the door, looked for signs for the operating theatre, found the recovery room and rushed in, just at the very moment that Maddy, her whiter than purest snow plaster-cast raised up on a frame, opened her bleary eyes and smiled.

While she lay in bed, plugged into bleeping apparatus and being diligently attended by a succession of nurses and doctors, I felt intensely guilty. Unlike her sister, she had not shown any enthusiasm for a skiing holiday but we had jollied her along, encouraging her to at least give it a go. If she really didn't like it, which of course we knew she would, there would be lots of other things to do in happy Hogfjells, such as sleigh rides and tobogganing. I cast around for others to blame for the accident. Maybe the ski hire shop had set the bindings incorrectly, perhaps the instructor had pushed her too hard. But there was really no explanation for the fracture other than a freak accident.

While Maddy was de-grogging, I asked a recovery nurse whether she skied, given the steady flow of breakages they have to deal with. 'Of course,' she said. 'Everybody I know who works in the hospital skis.'

'Ah, but I bet you don't ski fast,' I added.

'No, we do ski fast. But when you work in A&E, you always drive slowly.'

A PS

For the rest of the week Maddy made slow progress, mostly in bed with short practice 'runs' on crutches, spiked to bite into the ice on the sloping path between our cabin and the hotel's restaurant. Luckily the hotel was a very pleasant place to do very little.

With five suitcases, a barely mobile Maddy, her sister Francesca and her two-year-old brother Jonah, the return journey by train and plane was never going to be easy but we – my wife Charlotte and I – managed. Oslo airport, conveniently, had its own railway station. I had also called British Airways to make sure our invalid was recorded in the system, a suitable seat allocated and wheelchair waiting at Heathrow, and was reassured that all was in place.

So why am I telling you all this? To put you off skiing? I hope not. Thanks to advances in equipment, especially boot and binding design, as well as safety rules on the slopes, accidents are relatively rare. But the sport does carry risks, which is why you have to pay an additional premium on travel insurance.

While in hospital, I double-checked the small print in our annual cover, just to be sure that winter sports were included. They were. I then found out that, although not in the EU, Norway had reciprocal medical arrangements with the UK. The whole business, including the initial X-ray, two taxi rides of well over an hour each, plus waiting time, the full hospital works and crutches, which we posted back to Lillehammer three months later with a big thank-you note, had cost just £50.

13

LOBSTER TALES

Embossed on the car registration plates in Maine was the word 'Vacationland'. Now what could be more promising than that? It also showed a small pink lobster, designed to get our lips smacking long before we even saw the sea.

The seemingly infinite, ins and outs, coastline of Maine – 3,400 miles if you've left your tape measure at home – is the reason why a US state of 1.3 million inhabitants draws thirty-six million visitors a year. They come to sail it, fish it, paint it, stay in old sea captain's houses or simply treat their lungs to its tangy fragrance. And to eat lobsters. The place is crawling with them.

Even driving in Maine is all about the sea, hopping across Meccano-ish bridges from one inlet to the next, or detouring down long finger promontories which reach out like fish bones from the highway to the ocean. Sometimes people dare to swim in it, although even in summer it can feel chillier than the meltwaters of an ice bucket.

We – my wife Charlotte and our two girls (Cesca six, Maddy three) – rented a house in Boothbay Harbour which was built on legs which paddled in the sea and with a deck as broad as Brighton Pier. The interior looked like an aquarium in the advanced stages of rigor mortis. There were fish everywhere, pushing the children's I-spy score to the very limits of their counting skills. We had lobster pulls on light switches, lobsters on the cushions, fish breadboards and fish napkin rings, fish oven gloves, fish soaps, fish hob covers, crabs on the towels and, some nights, fish nightmares. Everything was themed except for a pair of elephants. And even they were made of tiny seashells.

This may be hard to swallow, but not so long ago Maine's world-famous crustaceans were used to fertilise the fields. Were you to eat the odd one or two, you made damn sure to hide the shells so as not to bring shame on the family. The archive of one state jail even records how inmates would complain when served lobster more than twice in a single week.

We ate lobster until we groaned, 'Never again.' We ate them at the Lobsterman's Coop, on a deck next to the boats, at the Fisherman's Wharf overlooking the Damariscotta river in a dining room decked out like an old ship. We had them on popovers, a distant cousin of the Yorkshire pudding, and we ate them in chowders. Many restaurants had table mats showing how to use a claw cracker and a long-pronged fork. We got so used to wearing bibs that we were on the verge of throwing tantrums when there was no Heinz baby mush for pudding, and couldn't understand why the Chardonnay came in a glass rather than a Tommy Tippy cup.

We also learnt how to catch one. We put to sea aboard *Miss Boothbay*, skippered by Dan Stevens. In Maine, they say, you need to have at least three generations in the ground before you can be considered a native; Dan, a fifth-generation fisherman, was fully qualified. We helped haul traps, measure the prisoners, toss back any that fell short of the legal minimum and fitted those destined for the pot with a pair of thick, elastic claw bands. 'Lobsters are all size eighty shirt and size ten hat,' said Dan, in an accent as flat as a clam bed at low tide. He meant all brawn but no brain. He showed us his scars, including a couple on his stomach where a female whopper grabbed him in a painful embrace. The girls screamed.

By the end of the week we had worked up enough confidence to buy a quartet of living lobsters, and cook them at home. I loaded the children into the house dinghy and rowed across Mill Cove to Wotton's Lobster Dock, my competence as an oarsman no doubt continuing a tradition noted by Jan Morris, on how 'Maine skippers were admired from the Elbe to the Amazon'.

We bought our supper, of four pound-and-a-halfers, and rode them back to base, hoping those elastic armbands wouldn't snap and send them scurrying about in the bottom on the boat in search of a tiny toe or two.

Crucial in our kitchen armoury was a bucket of a saucepan in which to cook them. We brought the water to the boil and immersed the critters with a pair of tongs. I felt my shoulders tense; my wife closed her eyes; the girls ran away. It began to feel like a chapter from a Hilary Mantel book come to life. But we not only survived but, drawing on our newly acquired claw and fork skills, we felt almost native.

14

WASHED ASHORE

We, the Wickers family, planned to spend one Christmas at the Anantara Hotel in Si Kao, a resort near Krabi on the Thai mainland. At the time, our three children were aged twenty-one (Cesca), eighteen (Maddy) and eleven (Jonah). Cesca and I had flown out ahead of the rest of the family to join a cruise, sailing from Singapore to Phuket. We were all to meet up at Phuket airport a week later and transfer to the Anantara by minibus.

One day, half-way through our cruise, the ship dropped anchor off an island called Koh Kradan, ten miles or so across the bay from Si Kao. Once Cesca and I had been tendered ashore, we decided to go for a long walk, half paddling, half strolling along the sands.

After a few minutes I spotted a large Anantara sign at the entrance to a white, beachfront building and experienced a moment of blind panic. Why was the Anantara here, on a tiny island, and not the mainland, as I was led to believe? Had I got it all wrong? Should I cancel the minibus? Did I need to arrange for a boat take us to Koh Kradan from Phuket?

The hotel had merely confirmed the booking, assuming that anyone getting to that stage in planning their holiday would at least know where their chosen accommodation was located and have made the necessary arrangements for getting there.

We stepped inside the Anantara to speak to someone in the hopes of trying to rectify the problem. The girl on the desk must have thought I was mad. 'We are staying here next week,' I explained, 'and I was wondering how we can travel here from Phuket.'

'No rooms here, sir,' she said. 'Only lunch.'

'Lunch? But this is the Anantara, yes?'

'Yes, it is the Anantara.'

'But our rooms are already booked. Under Wickers. Next week, not this.'

'But no rooms here, sir. This is the Anantara beach club.'

'Oh. So, er, where's the actual hotel?'

'On the mainland, sir. In Si Kao. South of Krabi. Every day a boat brings guests to our island for lunch on our beach. Maybe you come back next week?'

Confused? Moi? No more. I think Cesca was mightily relieved to learn that her father hadn't lost the plot after all.

We spent the rest of the time doing the usual beach stuff until it was time to make our way back to where the ship's tender would pick us up.

On the stroll back along the sands, we thought of a great trick to play on Jonah. We came across a tree trunk, bleached smooth and silver by its oceanic passage before being tossed ashore by a high tide or a storm. No doubt it would be washed away again in a matter of weeks, but that was unlikely to happen in the next few days (I emphasise that point before telling you what we did – I'd hate you to think we were a couple of nature vandals).

I always travel with my trusty Leatherman multi-function tool, even on a jaunt to a beach. You never know when it might come in handy, as in this very moment of inspiration. Cesca and I took turns carving 'Jonah Wickers', letter by letter, into the thick, meaty part of the trunk. It was a slow process, but we were pleased with the clarity of our artwork and stood back to admire it.

We then returned to the ship and continued the cruise, disembarking in Phuket and heading to the airport, where my wife Charlotte, along with Maddy and Jonah, were due to arrive in a couple of hours. We then all piled into a minivan, drove to Krabi and onto Si Kao, where we checked into the Anantara, mainland version.

On Boxing Day, we boarded the hotel's excursion boat and zipped across the water to Koh Kradan and the beach club. We didn't let on to the rest of the family that we'd been there the previous week. 'Hey, let's just take a stroll along the beach before we go swimming,' I suggested. Cesca and I made sure that we walked on either side of Jonah and made our way towards our arboreal artwork.

'Just look at that huge piece of driftwood, Jonah,' Cesca said. 'I wonder how far it has travelled before being thrown up on the beach? It looks so white from spending so long in the sea and the sun. And look, there's some writing carved on the side. My God, look! It says Jonah Wickers! That is absolutely incredible.'

'No it isn't,' said Jonah. 'You have obviously just written it.'

15

GOING WITH THE FLOW

It took just five minutes to realise that making a Swedish raft would be a lot harder than making a Swedish bookcase, at least one flat-packed by Ikea with a little poly bag containing nuts, an allen key and set of instructions. Our logs – and our lives – would be held together solely by ropes. 'Oh dear, I think that you will have a hard day tomorrow,' warned Bentoka, one of the base camp instructors, as he inspected our spaghetti of practice bindings.

We – two dads and our two nine-year-old children – were on day one of a summer rafting adventure on the Klaralven. From its source near the Norwegian border to the oceanic Vanern, the largest lake in Europe, the river snakes in boa-size meanders through the heart of Sweden.

We spent most of day one getting to the base camp, flying from London to Gothenburg and driving a rental car the 350 kilometres to Gunnerud, hometown of Vildmark i Varmland, which has been organising self-drive rafting trips on the river since 1980.

The base camp was little more than a cluster of wooden sheds filled with all rafters' needs (except the rafts – we'll come to them later). After checking in, we were handed six large plywood chests which we carted by trolley to a nearby meadow. We opened the one marked 'grund' and found two tents and a shovel for digging latrines, then opened the 'kok' box and made supper. It was then time, in the long late light of midsummer, for our lesson in lashing.

Bentoka worried us further. He showed us a map of the Klaralven and catalogued the hazards: whirlpools from which we may never get out, dead water that would get us nowhere, backward-flowing water, backward-moving raft (wind greater than current), overhanging trees that could wipe away an unsuspecting crew like a giant scythe, hidden rocks to ravage our bottom, bridge stanchions that could snap us in two and sandbanks that could Velcro us to a single spot for hours on end.

Thank you, Bentoka. I went to sleep thinking about Humphrey Bogart heaving the African Queen through leech-infested swamps and dreamt about being on a boat irresistibly drawn to the lip of a thundering waterfall.

Early the following morning we loaded our plywood toy boxes of gear onto a trailer and, along with four other rafting parties, climbed aboard a bus for the drive upstream. After an hour or so on the road we reached the launch site at Osebol, where an immense mountain of untethered pine logs stood beside the riverbank.

Some 'log-arithms'. Each log was three metres long and each raft is made up of three layers. Since each completed raft measures around six metres by three, it doesn't take a maths genius to work out that you need to build two square rafts, then bind them together into a single, river-friendly, life-preserving whole.

Rule one of raft making: do it in the water. This may not be obvious from where you are sitting, but there is no way you can move a finished raft from land to the water. We – dads, of course – struggled to carry one log at a time. In the end we managed to relocate a total of 160 logs from pile to river. No graft, no raft.

The riverbank soon began to resemble a medieval shipyard, with rafters beavering back and forth between the water and the pick-a-stick stack of logs, then donning thigh-high boots and wading into the shallows for essential rope work. The children sloped off to play mini golf in the nearby campsite while the dads slowly sank to their knees with fatigue. Thank heaven for Henrik, instructor and all-round hero, who helped with the last lashings and the piece-de-raft resistance, a Huck Finn of a canopy under which we would store equipment as well as ourselves when it rained (which it did – Varmland can be anything but a varm land even in summer).

We picked up a pair of long poles for punting, paddles for paddling and lifejackets for – well, best not think about their prospective role – and by 4pm our ship was ready for its maiden voyage.

We loaded the children on board, poled ourselves from the bank and nudged into the three kilometres per hour slipstream. At first, we thought we were in full control. We sat on either side of the raft and paddled, then paddled harder, but made not the slightest impression on our course. The only master of movement was the Klaralven, which took us and our two tons of logs wherever it wanted.

A raft is a craft with no power, no brakes and no steering. Once we had severed our ties to the bank, we simply became part of the river, a life-size bundle of Pooh sticks moving at exactly the same pace as the inky black water. It was a curious sensation. Toss an apple core into the river and it simply stays with you. The same when you pee off the side, an even more fascinating fact of science as far as the children were concerned.

For two hundred years the Klaralven was the busiest logging river in Sweden. Nowadays, the logs are transported on the backs of huge thundering trucks, leaving the Klaralven an empty ghost of an artery, a private wilderness for rafters and the occasional canoeist. In three days we saw no more than half a dozen fellow floaters.

We did, however, encounter several of Bentoka's dangers. Overhanging trees were a nuisance not a threat – except once when a branch completely demolished our canopy. Sandbanks were plenty, heralded by the sight of the river bottom suddenly looming below, just a foot or two between us and the rippled, rust-coloured riverbed.

Miraculously the river bore us clear of the sands but not a whirlpool. It had us slowly gyrating in circles, completely unresponsive to poling or paddling, so we just sat back and wallowed in helplessness. After around half an hour, like a cat playing with a dead mouse, the river got bored, cast us aside and back into the current.

Submerged rocks also caught us in mid-drift, buckling and twisting the raft as if it had been attacked by an undersea serpent. Our lashings held, just. By the end of the trip our midships were below the waterline but our bows and stern rode high and proud.

The Klaralven was our Amazon, our Orinoco. Most of the journey was deliciously uneventful, the woody, watery wilderness drifting peacefully by. Sometimes a village would ease past, its residents stopping to gaze and wave at our passing. With little to do apart from occasionally manning the poling stations, we dozed, daydreamed, played games, made tea, even cooked on board and generally adjusted to the natural order of things.

Since rafts move in silence, with, rather than through, the water, they are perfect vehicles for animal sightings. On one occasion we eased within a foot of a beaver before it suddenly looked up, a cartoon expression of shock horror writ large across its face, gave the surface of the water a great warning smack with its tail and submerged to freedom.

At night we camped ashore. Camping was the easy bit. The big problem was parking. With the momentum of a cargo ship, it was impossible to jump off the raft and stop it from disappearing without first taking a few turns of a rope around a tree. We spent the first night at a campsite. It was more a case of the campsite finding us because we just happened to be bouncing along the riverbank at the time and it simply got in the way. We lit a fire, cooked some odd-looking sausages from our *kok* supplies, had hot showers, used the loos and spoke in high praise of the Swedish outdoor lifestyle.

On the second evening we went wild, taking full advantage of the Swedish law which gives everyone the right to enjoy a one-night stand on any patch of land except a private garden or field of crops.

I got little sleep. Knowing how little control we had over the raft, how were we ever going to be sure of stopping back at the Gunnerud base camp? Miss it and we could well end up being tunnelled through a hydro-electric turbine, destined to help light the bedside lamps and dishwashers of the local Swedes?

We made it. Or, rather, the river happened to carry us to the right spot on the bank. We took down the tent and packed up our boxes, then the raft had a complete physical breakdown. Our final task before leaving the base was to untie every single knot and lashing and set the logs adrift, one by one, in the current. We speculated on their fate. Thousands upon thousands of matches? Pencils? Newspapers? Snooker cues? An Ikea bunk bed? Nothing of the sort. According to Bentoka (who, for some unaccountable reason, seemed very surprised to see us), there is a large net a mile or so downstream where the catch of the day is hauled out of the river and driven back to Osebol ready for the next lot of rafters.

With my hands like a rigger's, covered in minor cuts, callouses, sores and blisters, I could barely hold the car steering wheel for the drive back south. We followed the river to Karlstad for a last night in the Scandic Hotel. Rafting is a very grunge experience and were it not for having two nine-year-olds in tow I'm not sure if we would have passed the scrutiny of the doorman. After totally abusing the spotless bathrooms with our grime, we went to have one last look at the Klaralven, realising that we would never look at any river in quite the same way again. Nor a pine tree.

16

VIRGIN SAILORS

The still airs of the Caribbean night were shattered by an expletive from my friend Will. It was the shock of seeing the size of our yacht, all forty-eight feet of her with a beam as broad as a bus.

Charter boats in the Med, the only place we had previously sailed, are mostly of much smaller proportions. In the Caribbean, where Americans dominate the charter market, they come both big and well endowed. Ours, the good ship *Brustalon*, had three fridges, three cabins each with flushing loos, four showers (one on the aft deck for washing the salt off after a swim), a telephone as well as VHF and a barbecue. Even the tender could have passed as a minor landing craft.

We unpacked and went into Road Town, capital of the British Virgin Islands, for a quiet worry at Pussers, a theme park of a ye-olde-Englande tavern. A plate of shepherd's pie and a tot or two of rum, authentically distilled to Royal Navy specifications, restored confidence in our nautical skills.

So, too, did the fleet manager at the Stardust marina, Lieutenant Commander Tony Newling-Ward (RN retired). His briefing the next morning was as blustery as a Force 8. 'Basically, it's bloody dead easy,' was the commander's opening salvo. Pointing to a hand-painted chart of the Virgins on the wall, he ordered us to 'sail in white bits, steer clear of the red, anchor in the pink and drink in the blue'.

We pretended not to notice the bent mast laid out on the marina quay, a victim of a recent hurricane, the worst to hit the islands for 120 years. Several boats at other marinas were trashed, masts snapping like dry twigs, hulls splitting like peanut shells, decks splintering like pork scratchings. But we were here at the end of October, on the right side of risk season, and, barring a few topless palm trees and a high quota of shiny tin roofs, the islands seemed mostly back to normal.

Holidays in the BVIs are much more to do with seawater than rainwater. You can hop between islands by ferries, rent a paddle board, take a sunset cruise, dive to inspect wrecks and coral gardens, swim, snorkel, and, above all, sail. This dense seascape of islands – named by Columbus after St Ursula's team of 11,000 virgins – offers some of the best and certainly the easiest cruising waters in the Caribbean. They are the nursery slopes of yachting, with consistent but rarely forceful northeasterly trade winds and easy hops between several ports of call. Even the names on the charts – Dead Man's Bay, Fallen Jerusalem and Dead Chest where Blackbeard, aka Long John Silver, put his mutinous crew ashore with just a bottle of rum, yo ho ho – conjure up the ghosts of peg legs and swarthy sea dogs.

The islands, in fact, are something of a holiday oddity, a destination where the bulk of tourists never sleep a single night ashore. There are more yacht berths than hotel beds! Even restaurants keep a listening watch on the VHF channel so that mariners can make a reservation for dinner while still beating into the trades.

Scattered over miles of incomparably blue sea, the islands are steep and green, the peaks of a submerged chain of volcanoes. Britain and the United States meet right here, on a dotted frontier that perforates the chart. Just under half of the ninety-odd islands are a British Crown Colony, the rest an 'unincorporated territory of the USA'. We stuck to Britain, as indeed do most American yachties, since the sailing is more interesting, the anchorages more plentiful and the crime rate much lower.

Will and I – we had no other crew – did the standard, one week, anti-clockwise, BVI milk run and loved it. After stocking up and signing ship's papers we set sail, following the commander's advice to 'nip across to the Indians to blow out the cobwebs and enjoy a spot of bloody lovely snorkelling'. The Indians are the needles of the Caribbean, sharp pinnacles of rock growing from beds of coral and colonised by fish in their Sunday-best scales. We had to hang about for a while waiting for a mooring buoy – instant reminders of Saturday morning at the Sainsbury's car park. After a bloody lovely snorkel, we cooked spaghetti for lunch and fed the leftovers to a flash and a thrash of fish tails.

In the afternoon we sailed past Salt, where the brothers Herman and Norwell still panned and dried salt by hand, paying the islands' governor a bag a year as peppercorn rent. While I was on the helm, Will called the beach bar on Cooper Island to book our table for supper, anchoring in the lee of an outcrop called the Cistern.

Early the next morning (our body clocks still clinging to UK time), sipping our tea on the deck, we saw that the next-door yacht was adrift, dragging on its anchor and heading towards the Cistern's fangs like a doomed *Marie Celeste*. We launched a rescue mission, leaping into our tender but failing to start the outboard. A few pulls later it spluttered to life and we raced across the silvery dawn sea to the helpless craft like warriors on a Greenpeace sortie.

We banged on the side of the yacht's hull and nipped round to the stern to nose and nudge the yacht away from certain peril. A head popped up through the hatch, his face revealing an expression you'd probably reserve for the dawn of Armageddon. The head disappeared and resurfaced with a body, bare apart from undies. He fired his ignition and we were instantly Chernobyled by a cloud of noxious fumes, but our mission to seamen was accomplished. He chugged to safety, giving us a broad wave, just like the final sequence of a *Lone Ranger* episode.

Since we were up and kicked into life, we decide to get to the Baths, the number-one sight in the BVIs, before the crowds. The pinky grey, granite boulders, Dali rounded and as big as clouds, are the distinctive birthmark on the island of Virgin Gorda. We dropped anchor, swam ashore and had them almost to ourselves. We walked and waded, Indiana Jones-style, through a playground of grottoes, caves and seawater jacuzzis, before emerging on a white, silky beach and snorkelling back to the boat through a peppermint sea.

For lunch we clamped our barbecue to the aft rail, creating a flaming tail like some aquatic dragon; an alarming prospect but we burnt neither burgers nor *Brustalon*.

We sailed between the Dogs, not poodles but a mini archipelago, aimed for Branson's Necker and sharp turned to starboard along the channel markers to the Bitter End, the last point of land before reaching the open waters of the Atlantic.

Bitter End is a hotel but one so nautical it is almost a boat, with a sailing school, marina, mooring buoys and 150 boats for the use of guests. We came ashore for the week's best dinner, stopping off en-route at a tiny little islet called Saba Rock, where a shack of a bar, complete with parrot, came as close to a pirate's lair as you could find.

You can do the BVIs comfortably in a week, but you need more if you want to take an eighteen-mile detour to the coral, pancake-flat Anegada, a trickier sail partly because it is hard to spot until you almost run aground, and partly because of its enormous halo of reefs which has garrotted many a mariner. Our binoculars had developed mysterious cataracts so, not wanting to sail right past, next stop Newfoundland, we were secretly relived that time was against us.

Our October weather was both sulky and sunny, with fleecy wool clouds and the occasional squall when the sky suddenly looked as if someone had tipped a pot of ink over the ceiling. We usually saw them coming and could steer round the edges, but even when squalls scored a direct hit, the fierce rain, high winds and low visibility came and went within a few minutes.

Sailing in the Caribbean is a quest for Holy Grails. As well as charts and pilot book – the indispensable, annually updated *Yachtsman's Guide to the Virgin Islands* – all good sailors must pick up a copy of *Limin Times*, which lists all the week's events, from pig roasts at Ali Baba's to the big weekend barbecue at Foxy's. Despite their low-key, laid-back, tiny population, the BVIs have some remarkable nightlife. Many sailors navigate by bars rather than stars.

On the northern exposed coast of Tortola, film setting for *The Old Man and the Sea*, we set course for Cane Garden Bay and a night of pounding reggae at Quito's Gazebo. At Trellis Bay, after a couple of 'No See Um' cocktails at De Loose Mongoose, named after an American brand of midge and a definite danger to shipping, according to the commander, with 'a bite like a bastard and a kick like a horse', we tenderly tendered to the Last Resort for roast beef and Yorkshire pudding. In the middle of dinner, a donkey called Vanilla trooped unaccompanied right through the restaurant. And the cabaret, performed by owner Tony Snell, ex-artiste from the Windmill and star of *One Man Banned* at the Lyric in Jersey, hadn't even started.

17

THE WALK THAT NEVER WAS

Many years ago I wrote *Britain at Your Feet*, a book about backpacking on the UK's officially designated, long-distance footpaths, now called National Trails. It was co-written with my very good American friend and skilled outdoorsman Art Pedersen.

We walked miles, heaving our twenty-five- to thirty-pound packs loaded with camping and cooking gear, sleeping bags, dried foods including essential GORP (good old raisins and peanuts, laced with chunks of chocolate), spare clothing and other essentials. We followed the entire Pembrokeshire coast path, Offa's Dyke and the Ridgeway, took big bites out of the South West Way, hiked the Pennine Way from Edale to the Scottish border and the South Downs Way. Each was a star trek, an escape from traffic jams and people jams, the experience almost entirely rural.

Before starting the book, we contacted several manufacturers of outdoor gear to ask if they would sponsor us by providing various items of equipment. Their response was very enthusiastic. We test-drove tents, cooking stoves, sleeping bags and boots. In fact, we got so many boots that I gave one pair to my seventy-two-year-old dad. He had shown great interest in the idea of backpacking, at the time an activity barely known to Brits (hence the reason for writing the book).

I promised to take my dad on a two- or three-day jaunt, fairly close to home and nothing too demanding. I encouraged him to get in shape beforehand. He had suffered a heart attack five or six years previously and had given up smoking, apart from a pipe and the odd Manikin cigar at Christmas, but his retirement days had become mostly sedentary. So, I reasoned, some gentle preparatory exercise would be a good thing.

Dad took up the challenge. Living in a council flat in a tower block near Regents Park, he began a daily routine of leaving home before breakfast, wearing his new boots and walking a three-mile circuit of the Park's Outer Ring. As the weeks passed he would call regularly to update me on his progress, saying how he could now walk twice around the perimeter and that he was feeling in fine fettle and that his boots were fully broken in.

I'm ashamed to admit it but, in the selfishness of youth, I began to have second thoughts about the whole venture. I loved him dearly but worried that spending three full days together, sleeping in a small tent, could drive me bonkers. I stalled, urging him to keep up the training and, come the nice weather (it was still winter), we would do it. Or at least an edited version.

Towards the end of March Art and I, plus a couple of friends, walked a section of the South Downs Way over a weekend. We had left my car in the residents' parking below my parents' block of flats, caught a train to Eastbourne and set off along the path. The weather was glorious, the walk quite demanding because of the roller-coaster topography, but our spirits soared.

We came back to London around nine o'clock in the evening feeling happy but weary. Rather than call in to say hi to my parents, we went straight to the car which stood directly below the windows to their flat on the thirteenth floor. As we were loading up the boot I heard someone, a man, call my name. It didn't sound like my dad and all I could see in the dark was a head silhouetted by the light coming from their bedroom, but I presumed it must be him. The voice again called out, 'David, you'd better come up.'

I realised it wasn't my dad but my Uncle Fred. How strange. I asked the others to wait, moaned about the inconvenience, said I'd just be a couple of minutes and rode up in the lift. As the doors opened on the landing I saw Fred standing at the open flat door. I felt bad, thinking my dad must be ill and that I shouldn't have felt put out by the delay in getting back to my own flat. I then saw my mum, who was clearly upset. I walked straight into their bedroom, expecting to see my dad in bed with some nasty bug or bronchitis to which he was prone. The bed was empty.

I can't remember exactly how the news was conveyed, or who conveyed it, but the terrible fact was that my father had died. He had been found by passers-by lying on the pavement on the Outer Ring of Regents Park, and had been taken off by ambulance. He'd had a heart attack.

I'm not sure of the finer points of law but because he had died on the street, dad had to be identified. The next day I went, on my own, to the morgue and was taken to where he lay on a trolley, his facial features arrested in a moment of agony. I felt wrecked.

I confirmed his identity, thanked the mortician and walked out into the corridor. Someone called me back. 'Sorry, but you've forgotten these,' a woman said, handing me a grey, plastic bin bag. 'Your father's belongings.' I looked inside and saw, below his coat, jumper, trousers and a flat cap, the boots.

There had to be an autopsy, which confirmed a heart attack, a 'myocardial infarction'. I made arrangements for the cremation. The undertakers asked if we – my mother and I – wanted to see the body beforehand, which my mother was keen to do. My dad, just like Lenin, was lying in state, tucked into a cocoon of silky something. His face was not only made up like a mannequin, completely transformed from the one I saw on the morgue table, but bore a daft, inane smile. It was totally unlike the dad I knew.

My mum immediately broke down and lunged at the body, clearly intent on giving him a last hug. I dreaded the consequences, knowing that beneath that cover sheet would be a rather fragile, post-autopsified, deconstructed body that would probably react rather horrifically to a passionate embrace. I managed to grab her just before contact and ease her away.

Fast forward to the cremation. It always strikes me, as a classic example of the inequities of the British class system, that the only time most lower-income earners ever get to ride in a Rolls Royce is when they are dead. My mum and I followed the hearse in a second car, not a Roller. We had barely driven more than a couple of minutes when she turned to me and casually remarked: 'You've got keys to the flat, David, yes? Only I've left mine on the hall table.'

Oh dear. I hadn't even got a set of flat keys as the locks had been recently changed. And nor did any of the neighbours. Or the caretaker to the tower block. My dad's keys, which had been in the belongings bin bag, were also somewhere indoors. And the plan was for everyone going to the cremation to go back for tea, sandwiches and Victoria sponge cake, already laid out on the kitchen table.

When we drew up at the crematorium, I went up to one of the doleful attendants, told him the problem and asked if he could call his office during the ceremony and get them to contact a locksmith who, hopefully, would meet us at the flat on our return. He said not to worry, all would be taken care of.

I almost felt he was on the verge of adding, 'You go and enjoy yourselves.'

I won't go into details about the ceremony except to say it was conducted by a vicar who hadn't ever met my father but pretended to know him well. I felt I should be sobbing but it all seemed far too surreal. I also wanted to remain rock solid for the sake of my mum.

The small crowd drifted out. I told everyone we had to make a short stop at the funeral parlour (as such places used to be called, although there was nothing remotely parlour-esque about the place) and that we would see them at the flat. Our driver took us straight to the office. I asked the receptionist whether the locksmith had been sorted and she apologised. 'Oh no, sorry, we did try but couldn't get hold of one.'

We drove to the flat. On the landing, just outside the door, the various friends and relatives were waiting. Art was among them. He later told me that my wicked Aunty Nell had spread rumours that we were being detained by the undertakers because we didn't have enough funds to settle the bill.

Art and I discussed the problem. Art was wearing his favourite and familiar (and maybe only) footwear, a pair of heavy-duty walking boots that had also been supplied by the same company as my dad's pair. We decided that our only option was to kick the door open and deal with the consequences later.

My mum suddenly remembered she had the telephone number of the caretaker with her. I called him from one of the neighbour's, he explained the problem and moments later he turned up waving a metal coat hanger. 'I've had this problem a couple of times before,' he told us. 'These new locks are useless. Anyone can break in. I must have told the council a hundred times they need to change them.'

In less than five minutes he managed to work the lock open via the letter box and we all went in for tea, sandwiches and Victoria sponge cake.

A couple of weeks later, leaving my mum in the care of a relative (not Nell), Art and I went off to Wales on another backpacking jaunt. Somewhere along Offa's Dyke, on a beautiful late April day, windy but with bright sunshine, blue skies and just a few scurrying clouds, we stopped for a GORP break beside a field and watched scores of newly born lambs dancing comical arabesques, their elders grazing and bleating contentedly. Suddenly a shadow from one of the clouds passed over the scene, blotting out the sunshine and chilling the air. That was the first time, but not the last, that I burst into tears.

18

IMPERFECT STORM

The kids could not believe their good fortune. Arriving at the marina near Split in Croatia, they discovered that the name of the yacht we had chartered for our two-week sailing holiday was *Never Never Land*.

There were four children in all, aged ten, seven, four and one (three siblings and a cousin), plus four parents.

Knowing we carried such a young cargo, the charter company, Sunsail, had taken the trouble to fit safety netting that ran all around the decks. We looked like a floating playpen, which was hardly in keeping with the swarthy, sea dog image I was cultivating, but as long as nobody started calling me Tinkerbell, all would be fine.

There are sailors who thrive on long, howling passages across empty oceans. And there are those who like a succession of short, breezy hops that fit neatly between late breakfasts, frequent swims and a nice piece of grilled fish and wine on a pretty quayside at the end of the day. We definitely fall into the latter category, especially with children whose sea-time threshold is invariably limited.

Our two-week, light pixie dusting aboard *Never Never Land* produced a full set of fabulous places. We sailed to the UNESCO World Heritage town of Trogir, a perfectly preserved outpost of the Venetian empire's 500-year dominance of these shores; to Stari Grad, which looks like a mini Dubrovnik; across to the island of Hvar, the 'Madeira of the Med'; and up the Skradin river to the Plitvice Lakes National Park.

We also went to the Kornati, a National Park wilderness made up of around 100 virtually deserted islands. Bedazzled by their beauty, George Bernard Shaw reckoned that God, wanting 'to crown his work, created them out of tears, stars and breath'. Although little more than a couple of hours' flight from London, sailing among this barren, biscuit-coloured archipelago, made us feel like latter-day Thor Heyerdahls.

One late afternoon we sailed into a well-protected bay, perfectly sheltered from the light, prevailing breeze. We dropped anchor, took the dinghy ashore and climbed to the top of a peak to take photos of our lonely craft floating upon the mirror-still waters.

There was no other boat to be seen, nor any sign of human habitation. When we returned to the yacht, a fisherman puttered up in his boat to sell us freshly caught calamari, his wife acting as a human grappling hook on our beam, keeping both boats together while the deal was done.

We cooked the calamari, drank wine and lounged around the deck in a blissful stupor, admiring the blanket of stars and feeling that life could not get any better. In fact, it was to get a lot worse.

In our haze of well-being we almost forgot the daily ritual of tuning into the local radio station for the 9pm weather forecast, broadcast in English. It had always been as comforting as a night-time cup of Horlicks, but not on this particular night. 'Warning to all ships at sea,' crackled the voice over the

VHF. 'Storm imminent. Gale-force winds expected from the south.' Our yacht, in its beautiful bay, was protected against all likely winds, apart from the freak occurrence of anything treacherous blowing in from the south.

Within an hour of the broadcast, the wind opened its throttle. Waves began to slap against our hull and the boat slewed round on its anchor which, given the sudden ferocity of the wind, was in danger of dragging and pushing us onto the shore. We had, we felt, no choice but to haul up our anchor and motor out of the bay into more open waters.

One huge downside about sailing in a wonderfully remote corner of the Med is the complete lack of navigation lights to guide us through the menacing teeth of the islands. Our only option was to spend the entire night slowly motoring up and down a mile or so of water which we knew, from our previous scrutiny of the chart, was safe. We didn't even have a sat nav on board – this was well before they became standard issue on charter boats – so we steered by the compass, taking it in turns to peer into the black night to make sure we didn't get too close to land.

With the sea now a foaming frenzy and the rain lashing in horizontal spears, the experience became increasingly exhausting as the hours passed. As first light appeared and the land began to be distinguishable against the pewter-grey sea and the sky, we decided to make for the only marina in the Kornati. The wind was still fierce but the rain was easing, the clouds gradually clearing and the sun began to blaze. It was going to be a beautiful day.

It took well over an hour to reach the marina. Although we had not seen a single boat during our passage, the marina was full. As we approached, a few of the early risers stood on their decks, mugs of tea and coffee to hand, wondering where we might have come from and why, given the savage weather, we would have chosen to be anywhere other than the marina. Many of the onlookers were already in swimwear, while we were still chilled to the bone and swaddled in all our outer layers as if we'd just sailed from Spitsbergen.

Tying up, with a strong wind blowing right across the side of the yacht, was a tricky manoeuvre. We needed to approach stern first, pick up a line attached to the quayside and secure it round a cleat in the bows before the wind smacked us into a neighbouring boat.

We managed it, the bow rope cleated and lines ashore tied with the help of a couple of yachties on the quayside. But moments before everything was finally secured, the engine still ticking over in neutral, our ten-year-old daughter Francesca, who was standing in the cockpit, tripped and fell onto the engine's gear lever, pushing it into reverse. The engine revved, the boat edged towards the jetty and the propeller passed over a shoreline which immediately snagged, wrapping itself around the prop shaft, stalling the engine. Oh dear.

There was only one way to resolve the problem and that was for me to strip off, don a mask and flippers, get into the water, and try to untangle the mess. The operation was both exhausting and scary because I had to swim right under the fat belly of the hull to reach the prop.

It proved impossible to free the line so I had to use a knife to cut it and then, with only seconds before the wind would push us hard against the next boat, rapidly tie the loose ends together.

Job done, I climbed back on board, shivering with cold, disappeared below decks, towelled myself down, put on two or three dry layers and a woolly hat, crept under a duvet in the cabin, and immediately fell into the deepest sleep. Two hours later I woke up feeling totally, and bizarrely, fully refreshed.

It was not until several weeks later that I discovered, just after I had gone below, that Francesca, not appreciating the impact of what she had done, had told her Aunty Liz that she felt 'really proud to have caused all this'.

'Ah,' said Liz, 'perhaps you'd better not tell your dad that. Not for a while anyway.'

Francesca has since become a fully qualified sailing instructor.

19

THE DEEP END

Although barely known, the island of Andros in the Bahamas is the fifth largest in the Caribbean. From the air it looks like an enormous doily, a green canvas of bush, mangrove and tropical forest, pitted by umpteen lagoons, creeks, bights and swamps.

I came as part of a round-up I was writing to show some of the difference between the various 'Out Islands' of the Bahamas. Bimini, for example, is best known for deep-sea fishing, the Abacos for sailing and Andros, whose fringing coral reef stretches for 100 miles along the entire length of the island, is famous for diving.

But first, a back story. A year prior to going to Andros, I visited Sri Lanka. One evening I was having dinner on my own at the historic Galle Face Hotel on the seafront in Colombo. A man and woman were dining on the next table. We started to chat, about the hotel, about the island, the food and the like. The woman then kindly suggested I join them at their table.

'I've always hated having dinner on my own,' she added. 'It's the worst thing about travelling solo.'

I thanked them, moved across and a waiter laid a third place. 'Have some wine,' the man offered; his accent and blond, blue-eyed looks, suggested a Scandinavian. He lifted the bottle from the ice bucket, poured me a glass and ordered another. Introductions were made. Michelle was an American, now living Los Angeles. Erik, a Norwegian, was from Bergen but now also living in California.

They had been in Sri Lanka for a couple of weeks and were flying to the Maldives early the following morning. Such was their enthusiasm, for the gorgeous, pearly white beaches and the incredible diving, that I was quite tempted to change plans and add a few days on whichever island they were heading. If I could get on a flight, Erik said, I'd be really welcome to join them. However, since I'd only recently arrived in Sri Lanka and had already made plans to explore, I felt it was too late in the day to change things.

After we'd finished the second bottle of wine, Erik stood up and announced that he was off to bed, wanting an early night because of their dawn flight. I also stood up, shook his hand, thanked him for the wine and fun evening, and turned to Michelle, offering my hand and wishing her safe travels. She took my hand, held it, but remained seated, making no attempt to move. Only when Erik had left the room did Michelle stand and, still holding my hand, led me out of the room.

'Erik and I are just friends, not lovers,' she explained as we strolled through the foyer up a flight of stairs and along a corridor to a room, her room. 'Let's smoke a joint,' she suggested, opening the door.

We spent the next three or four hours in bed.

At around three in the morning Michelle looked at her travel alarm clock, turned, kissed me softly and said: 'I think I really ought to get a couple of hours' sleep before heading to the airport.' I eased myself from the bed, dressed and we wished each other a fond farewell. As I opened the door, two members of staff, in bright white jackets, almost fell into the room before scurrying away. They had clearly been listening to the nocturnal goings-on. I went straight to my room. The following day I continued with plan A.

To Andros, a year or more away from Colombo. I arrived on an early flight from Nassau and took a taxi to a waterfront lodge, then the only place to stay on the island. At reception, the check-in formalities included filling out a form listing my diving qualifications and previous experience. Having only recently qualified as a PADI diver, with just two dives post-course in my log book, I planned to sign up for an easy-ish dive during my two-night stay, just to see what all the fuss was about.

My room wasn't yet ready so I made my way onto the terrace, where breakfast was still being served. I ordered. A few minutes later, as I was about to tuck into my eggs and bacon, a voice from behind said, 'David?' I turned, saw a woman who I recognised but couldn't, at that moment, recall who she was. She then said, 'It's Michelle. We met in Sri Lanka. My husband George and I own the lodge. I know you've only just arrived, but I do hope you'll like it here.'

Ah, yes, Michelle! George then wandered over. 'Hi, Dave. I hear you two met once before. In, where was it, darling, oh yes, Sri Lanka, when you went last January. I couldn't get away then – too frantic here. Great to have you, Dave. I've just put your name down for today's dive. I know you're going to love it. I'll probably catch you later but if not, see you at noon on the jetty.'

Wow! Well, he didn't punch me or appear anything other than cool, so I don't know what he knew about our 'met once before', but I wasn't planning to ask.

I finished breakfast, went to my room, unpacked and wandered across to the bar, hoping to grab another coffee. There was a small blackboard with the day's dive chalked up. It read: 'Today's the day we'll all come alive. It's over the wall to 185.' My name was the first of four on a list immediately below the ditty.

Another guest, an American, came and stood beside me, reading the note. 'Hey, sounds cool. You a dive fanatic too?'

'Not really,' I confessed. 'Only just got my PADI open water. I've only done a couple of shallow dives since. My name's down here but not really sure what it all means.'

'What? You gotta be kidding. Today's dive is going over the edge into TOTO.'

'TOTO?'

'Tongue of the Ocean. It's a god-awesome trench, a 6,000-foot gorge. It's where the reef disappears over a wall. You ever seen the Grand Canyon?'

'Yes, last year, as a matter of fact.'

'Well, TOTO is the ocean equivalent. But the dive is to 185 feet. That's way deep, my friend. I've been diving for five years and never gone deeper than 100 feet. My name's Wayne, by the way. I also know those other two dudes,' he said, pointing to the list. 'Bob and Anna. We're all from Oregon. So that means you must be Dave.'

'Yep, that's me. David, in fact. Pleased to meet you, Wayne.'

We shook hands. 'Sure thing. But hear me out here. I think this dive is way, way beyond your comfort zone. In fact it's way, way beyond the reach of most regular divers. Think about it. It ain't too late to bag out. You'd be doing yourself a favour. Anyway, see you later, Dave. Good meeting you.'

'Yeah, thanks. You too. And thanks for the advice. I'll see if George's around. He's obviously unaware of my lack of experience.'

I looked around for George and was told that he and Michelle were off fishing somewhere and wouldn't be back till around noon. I thought about rubbing my name off the board but decided I'd first straighten things out with one of the dive team. Why, I fretted, had George put me down for the deep

TOTO dive when the form I had completed on arrival had specifically asked for my diving experience?

I decided to go for a swim, dunking into the sea from a ladder on the jetty. On my return I was met at the top of the ladder by a large man wearing a grey wetsuit, with various items of diving equipment – tanks, weight belts, BCD (Buoyancy Control Device), wetsuit, etc. – at his feet. 'Hi. You must be Dave. I've got some kit here for you so let's get you prepped.'

I tried to explain how I thought it best if I didn't take part but Ben, the resort's dive master, said that George was keen for me to experience the Andros wall and that my presence was needed for the 'buddy' set-up. In other words, I would be partnered up with one of the other guys on the list, standard diving procedure.

The three Americans turned up, wearing or carrying all the kit plus what looked like some sophisticated dive accessories. 'Hey, good buddy Dave,' said Wayne. 'Didn't expect to see you on this outing. Thought you managed to talk to George about giving TOTO a miss.'

Just I was about to say how I hadn't seen him, George bounded in, all geared up and raring to go. 'Hey, Dave, let's get you kitted out. Any idea what you should be carrying on your weight belt? Don't want you shooting up to the surface like a ping-pong ball.'

'Hi, George. Hold on a sec. I really don't think I should do this dive. It's far too deep. Did you see my completed check-in form, with the details of my lack of experience?'

'I did but that won't be a problem. We'll all be together. You can buddy up with Wayne. And besides, we'll have Ben here in the boat. Ben will follow us down after securing a spare tank, just in case any of us run out of air. And you guys all need to know this. The tank will be suspended at around thirty feet, which is where we'll be stopping on the ascent to acclimatise.'

'But George—' I protested.

'All in a day's work. This dive is as routine for us as you Brits catching one of your big red buses to work. You'll be fine. And just imagine, a 185 dive in your log book is SO cool.'

I looked to Wayne for back-up but he was clearly psyching himself up for the dive, as were his pals.

'George, maybe I should—'

'So, Wayne, you'll buddy up with Dave here…'

'Sure thing,' agreed Wayne, giving me a wink.

'Bob and Ann can pair up,' George continued, 'and I'll lead the way. When we drop anchor we'll all make our way down the chain until we touch the seabed, regroup and then you'll all follow me to the edge and on we'll go. Max bottom time, two minutes. Stick together and let one another know if you feel anything but fantastic. Then we'll work our way back up to the surface, with two pit stops along the way, one at the spare tank. So, my band of brothers, and sister, let's go dive.'

I know, I know, I know… I should have stood my ground but I somehow got swept along by the group's gung-ho momentum and, once kitted out, stepped in the boat. We motored about a quarter of a mile offshore, with silent Ben at the helm, dropped anchor, checked our masks, inflated our BCDs and tipped backwards into the water.

We all bobbed on the surface before releasing the air in our jackets and slowly descended, following the anchor chain. I was the last to begin the descent. Half-way down I realised my borrowed mask was leaking. I stopped, readjusted and carried on down.

I could clearly see the group hovering around where the anchor had embedded and headed towards them. Rather than wait, George set off, followed by the other three. This is a big no-no for diving. Sticking together, at least with your assigned buddy, is a golden rule. And the dive leader, the daddy goose, should always be aware of his goslings.

I followed as fast as I could, fins flapping, but didn't manage to claw back their twenty-yard or so lead. Suddenly the four completely vanished. I swam in what I thought was their direction, at a depth of around forty feet, and then the seabed completely disappeared. Not only had the divers vanished but so had the world. I'd come to the edge of the abyss, the subaquatic equivalent of stepping off the cliff edge at Beachy Head, except that there was absolutely nothing to see other than the deepest, darkest blue.

I was terrified. I began to hyperventilate. I somehow managed to reclaim a measure of calm and considered my one option – to slowly return to the surface and hope that I could see the boat, or that Ben could see me. I turned and looked back up to the surface. As soon as I got my bearings, I saw Ben swimming towards me like a fat grey seal. He came right up to me, peered into my mask and we went through a silent chorus of divers' hand signals – you OK, sort of, do you want to go back up or do you want to go down into TOTO? With you? Yes. OK.

So, I, we, did it. We dived over the edge, straight down the cliff, head first and deeper and deeper until we came to a narrow shelf in the cliff and stopped. I looked along the wall of rock and saw, maybe 100 yards away on the same level, George and the others, their trail of tiny ascending bubbles appearing no bigger than champagne fizzing in a glass.

We stayed a very short time and began our ascent, making the necessary stops to avoid dangerous nitrogen narcosis, or the bends, with a final pause, at the air cylinder suspended by the rope like a hanged man. I checked the air in my own cylinder and saw I still had enough to get back to the boat.

On the ride back to the lodge, I sat in silence while the others high fived and emitted whoops of joy. I did feel an inner whoop or two but I also felt a lot of other things. Why had George encouraged me to go on the dive? Why had he, and the others, abandoned me at the bottom of the anchor chain? Had Michelle told him of our night in Colombo? Did he deliberately want to terrify me as sweet revenge for making love to his wife? Did he want to kill me?

Well, I never found all the answers but he certainly failed in the last, if that was his intention, but super succeeded in the first, scaring the trunks off me. At dinner that night, my last night, the four of us were each given a certificate of congratulation on our achievement. I never did see either George or Michelle ever again, but I did learn, by a chance reading somewhere, that George himself died in a terrible diving accident, trying to beat his own world record for the deepest dive.

20

CAVE DWELLING

The coral reefs that lie off the string of islands, or *cayes*, along the coast of Honduras offer some of the world's finest diving. As a newly qualified diver, with just the basic PADI Open Water certification, I was keen to add to my almost virgin log book. Having checked into a resort on Ambergris Caye, the largest island, I checked with the dive centre if I could go on the next guided dive. Of course, they said. I showed them my paperwork, completed the health and safety forms, signed on the dotted line, and turned up at the jetty the following morning.

Three others were booked on the same dive. It was immediately apparent that they were old hands at sub-aquatics. Not only did they have their own equipment, rather than borrowed from the resort, but they carried such serious accessories as wrist band computers, underwater cameras and hefty torches.

Torches? That should have conveyed something, but it

didn't. Along with the dive master and a boatman, we boarded a nippy Zodiac and cast off. After a few minutes, the boatman cut the motor and our guide, Miguel, tossed an anchor over the side. Turning to the four of us he explained what was about to happen. His briefing went more or less as follows.

'As you know' (I didn't) 'we are going to experience one of our famous cave dives. Once we are in the water, we'll follow the anchor rope down to about fifteen metres and then, all together, we will go over the wall, down into the trench. In another few metres we will see the opening to the cave. It is very small, a hole in the wall, maybe one metre wide.'

'When we are ready, I will go first and everyone should follow me, one by one. It is narrow and very dark inside but you all have good torches. We will swim along the narrow passage for about twenty metres, before turning to the right for another twelve or fifteen metres. After that you will see daylight again. You will be able to look up and see the surface. It will be very nice. We will swim along the canyon for maybe fifty metres and then slowly ascend to the surface, where Alfonso will be waiting for us in the boat.'

Dark? Narrow? One at a time? Torches? Should I bow out now, make some excuse about feeling nauseous or whatever and stay in the boat with Alfonso or…?

Miguel turned to me. 'Ah, you do not have a torch. That is a problem.'

'Yes, sorry, didn't realise. Perhaps I can go back…'

One of the other divers, a German, came to my rescue, or to the rescue that I really didn't want. '*Kein Problem*. I have second torch. Here, please borrow it to me.'

'Thank you, *danke schon*,' I muttered feebly. My escape with dignity was no longer an option even though the torch, compared to the heavy-duty versions my companions carried, was about the size of a fountain pen.

We went into the water, evacuated the air from the BCDs (buoyancy control devices) and followed our leader down the anchor chain. So far so good, although my heart was thumping and I was anxious that, at the rate I was breathing, my tank would run out of air before returning to the surface.

At the wall, where the continental shelf made a vertical dive into the deep, we headed, literally, head first, down the cliff face until we came to what looked like a hole no broader than a dustbin lid. I decided to be first in line after Miguel, sticking as close to his flippers as I possibly could, even though this meant having to nudge my German light sponsor out of the way to get into prime position.

My touch emitted the feeblest of beams, barely able to pick up the day-glo orange of Miguel's fins. I also had another worry: staying horizontal, neither letting my body drift up so that my tank would scrape the rock above, or down and risk grazing my knees on the bottom of the passage. Or, worse still, becoming wedged. I was glad that two of the three Germans were XL size.

We came to the bend in the pipework and I managed the kick turn without losing sight of Miguel. I began to relax a little. At one point I turned the torch to the side, the beam alighting on the eye of a big fish just inches away. I'm not sure who was more shocked, but at least he/she had the advantage of being able to dart away with a flick of a tail.

At the point where the tunnel opened to reveal daylight, I felt elated. The sight was amazing, the sunlight shafting down in heavenly rays, the sides of the canyon reaching up like the walls of some immense cathedral. It was glorious. And I was alive.

The rest of the dive was just as it was supposed to be. We slowly, safely, surfaced and there was Alfonso to help us back into the boat. In fact, the whole expedition was just as it was supposed to be. It was just me who had not been as I was supposed to be.

21

LEARNING CURVES

Holidays imply all sorts of good things – warm seas and sandy beaches, fancy food and wine, stunning scenery and historic sights. But how about one that promises a 'miraculous transformation'? A week of yoga, I was assured, would be like clearing a blocked drain. The emotional pain that I have supposedly been repressing for years would lift from my shoulders. I would feel so relaxed they would have to peel me off the floor. I was told I might even burst into tears.

I was certainly the perfect candidate. Or, rather, the imperfect candidate. I was in my mid-fifties and reasonably fit but as supple as a goal post and stiffening up by the minute. I have never been able to touch my toes; in truth, I could barely get past my knees. My wife said my posture was awful. 'A good stretching would do you good.'

Yoga in the sun was even more tempting. The course was to take place on the uncrowded, crinkle-cut, north-east coast of Corfu. But what would the other people be like? The last thing

I needed was to find myself drawn into a touchy-feely coven of New Ageists and I definitely had no plans to return home with a funny new name and a craving for twig tea.

Except for a builder called Terry, my fifteen fellow stretchers were all women, drawn from a variety of backgrounds and included a lawyer (specialising in medical negligence cases, handy should I snap in two while being shoehorned into an ambitious posture), a probation officer, a pair of healers who began to 'om' in a corner at the first night's drinks do, a housewife and a theatre director. Several already knew each other from a local yoga club. Some had also been on the same course the previous year when the only male had disappeared after the introductory session and was not seen for the rest of the week. His trousers had fallen down with the very first posture and he was too embarrassed to show his face again. Or his glutes.

There were two two-hour sessions a day, one in the morning, the other in the late afternoon. Our ground was billeted in apartments in and around the village of Agios Stephanos, but convened at an old villa above the glinting sea. Here we rolled out our mats on the terrace and moved through a range of postures under the guidance of Hilary Reem. She could have bent herself into a shoebox but was very gentle on less flexible beings. I especially liked her because she let me use props ('David, perhaps you'd better get a chair for this one,' or, 'David, maybe a couple of extra blocks would help?').

Although I was the only beginner, and still the star stiff at the end of the week, I felt neither inhibited nor humiliated even when others around me were contorting into pretzels. Yoga is not supposed to be comparative anyway, but it certainly helped that the others were such a friendly, uncompetitive bunch.

After a week I could do the downward dog, with almost straight legs, the tree of life without toppling, the warrior whilst looking across the sea to Albania and the crocodile without giggling. I even managed to do things in Sanskrit I can't even pronounce, surely the supreme test of body over mind? More esoteric goals, however, like separating my skin from my bones, completely eluded me. On one occasion, when we were asked to imagine a lotus flower opening on the top of our heads, I found myself worrying that my loose change would roll out of my pocket and down the terrace drain.

An underlying principle of yoga is to help counter the normal over-activity of the mind and the under-activity of the body. The relaxation period at the end of each session was devoted to the under-activity of both. Hilary's gentle, soothing words were so hypnotic that I usually nodded off. And snored.

In between sessions we did our own things: swam, walked, rented motorboats, enjoyed long lunches and shopped for breakfasts at the grocer which straddled the cultural divide between Kensington and the Ionian by stocking muesli and semi-skimmed, as well as open tubs of yoghurt and honey straight from a beehive which sat on top of the counter.

After the week, I returned home a bendier as well as a browner person. There were no tears and I was pleased to report that my trousers stayed up the entire time.

22

KIND HEARTS AND CASTANETS

Home to fiestas and flamenco, bullfights and strumming guitars, tapas and gazpacho, olives and oranges, fiery colours, and a searing summer heat, Andalucia is arguably the most Spanish part of Spain.

But how could I tap into the essence of this iconic region? Rather than simply going to Andalucia and taking a leisurely overview, might there be a way to take part in the performance instead of simply sitting in the audience?

By chance I came across an answer: a one-week course in flamenco, one of the 'most gigantic creations of the Spanish people' according to Federico Garcia Lorca. The course was to be taught in English in the historic heart of Granada, the last stronghold of the Moors before they were evicted by the Catholic monarchs.

As far as the origins of flamenco go, the jury is still out, although the common consensus is that it is the music and movement of underdogs, of Muslims, Jews and gypsies persecuted by the repressive Reis Catolicos. It became a defiant outlet for their thwarted passions.

Whatever it is, whoever you are, whenever and wherever you see it, flamenco strikes deep chords. If it feels lukewarm you are being taken for a ride – and are perhaps watching a show somewhere along the Costa del Sol (despite belonging to Andalucia, this overdeveloped strip of shoreline is as far from Granada as the dark side of the moon). More to the point of my tale, in Granada you can not only hear flamenco and see flamenco, you can dance flamenco.

I was late for my first lesson. On my drive from the airport I became lost in the narrow, twisting, cobbled alleyways of the Albaicin, the old gypsy quarter. After cursing the Moors for their inability to predict the future needs of a Ford Focus, I asked a taxi to lead the way.

My course was based at the Escuela de Flamenco Mariquilla, a hundred-year-old dance school owned by one of Spain's foremost divas of dance. I parked, stepped inside and followed the sound trail. I climbed a broad flight of stairs, overlooked by a gallery of dark, faded oil paintings of famous dancers, and stepped into the studio.

Two rows of women in flamboyant, traditional flamenco dresses were dancing, facing an entire wall of a pitted and pot-marked mirror, stomping thunderously on the boards as if throwing a tantrum at my late showing. I was the only male in the group. I stood at the back, struck what I thought was a suitably arrogant pose (previously rehearsed in front of the bathroom mirror), wore my best 'don't mess with me' expression and thumped around the room like a wounded hippo, desperately trying to absorb the rhythm.

The music stopped, the teacher said '*bienvendios*', everyone turned and all I could think of by way of introduction was to apologise for wearing jeans, a T-shirt and the wrong shoes. I should have invested in a pair of nifty, Cuban-heeled stompers instead of prancing about in trainers. It was like trying to play tennis with a paella pan.

My teacher, twenty-two-year-old Ana Cali, was one of Granada's top gypsy queens, a prodigy of the legendary Mariquilla who had made her first TV appearance at the age of nine. Her boyfriend, the gaunt but smiling Emilio Maya, played the guitar.

Ana's moves were mesmerising. Even her tiny hands, with or without castanets, seemed to dance whenever she demonstrated the moves (one evening, in the apres-school bar next door, I watched her take a Pringle from a box in an equally balletic movement between her thumb and index finger).

It took the ten of us, all beginners, an entire week to master just one, simple, choreographed routine. Flamenco isn't easy. The beat is complicated, the steps more so. Lord of the Dance I was not. I was the worst in the class by far, but I would not have missed a minute of my daily two-hour lessons.

Other activities were arranged as part of the course. We were taught the art of the '*compas*', not a means of navigating the city's alleyways, but the name of the rhythmic flamenco clapping. We had a lesson in salsa, another in *sevillanas*, a jollier, more frivolous version of flamenco. I also arranged a tango lesson with the outrageously beautiful Marta from Argentina, whose grandmother had first taught her the steps. She passed on one essential edict – 'never must any light pass between the body of the man and the woman'. This I found rather difficult, especially since Signor Marta, who shared the teaching with his wife, was supervising the lesson.

Out of school there was the whole of Granada to discover, its magnificent architecture topped by the Alhambra, the most glorious shrine to the Moors' exquisite aesthetics, and the Generalife Gardens, curated and nurtured to recreate paradise on earth. There were pretty squares, fountained courtyards, patios and wrought-iron balconies laden with flowers, the snow-capped peaks of the Sierra Nevada friezing the horizon.

As a card-carrying flamenco student you get to walk the streets of Granada with a proprietorial air. I may have looked the klutz in front of that pitted mirror but out and about I walked tall, with a click to my step and attitude writ large across my face.

There's a range of flamenco venues in town, from formal theatres to smoky tapas bars with stages no bigger than a tablecloth (one barman alternated between serving sherry, fancy clapping and clearing away the empties).

I visited the famous cave venues in the Sacromonte Hills, home to the city's all singing and dancing gypsy queens. In what is now a UNESCO World Heritage Listed neighbourhood, the clatter of castanets, tormented singing and strumming guitars seemed to seep from every pore, devouring the jasmine air.

I saw Miguel Angel Rojas dance as if suspended above the floor by an invisible thread that freed his legs from their mundane roles as body props. He not only defied gravity but moved at a pace so ferocious that showers of perspiration flew from his hair on each twist and turn of his head and into the front rows of the audience. Not unlike a dog shaking dry after a swim.

As I type these memories on my keyboard, I remember the words of praise from the spectators. '*Ole*,' they cried, '*viva la maquina escriber*,' meaning 'long live the typewriter', referring to the Gatling gun speed that his heels hit the floor (and not the pace of my keyboard tapping).

23

PILGRIM'S PROGRESS

Three fingers of land, shaped like Neptune's trident, point south from the mainland coast of Halkidiki, the north-east shoulder of Greece. Two of them, Kassandhra and Sithonia, are fairly typical of the rest of the Mediterranean shores, with hotels, campsites, tavernas, bars and cafes that serve *Tag Fruhstuck* – breakfast all day – to the predominantly German-speaking tourists.

Mount Athos, the third prong, is named after its highest mountain. It is, with the exception of much of Albania and North Africa, the last wholly undeveloped stretch of coastline on the Med. It is a republic of monks, a community of monasteries that has chosen to isolate itself from the secular world. Women are still banned by ancient edict of the Emperor Constantine in 1060. Even female animals are forbidden. Only twelve foreigners a day are granted a permit to visit the republic. I applied for one and received it a few weeks later.

At the tiny port of Ouranopolis, I nearly missed the morning ferry, the one specified on my permit, to Mount Athos. It had cast off twenty minutes early, leaving a fist-waving, saints-cursing band of unhappy pilgrims stranded on the jetty. An on-board official with a corporal's stripe checked my passport and scrutinised my *diamonitirion*, my permit entitling me to four nights' monastic hospitality.

We sailed for nearly two hours along the western, bony shore of Mont Athos, passing three of the twenty monasteries, including the giant Panteleimon, home since the twelfth century to twenty Russian monks. Topped by bulbous domes and rows of cells agape like empty eye sockets, it is one of the finest examples of Byzantine architecture in Europe. The Athos monasteries used to be home to 20,000 monks but fewer than 2,000 now live on the peninsula.

Once we had docked at the tiny harbour of Daphne, I joined a group of pilgrims trying to squeeze onto a bus several sizes too small for its eager cargo. Tempers, elbows, hats and spectacles flew, all belonging to men just two hours into their temporary celibacy.

I managed to clamber aboard and sat on a broken spring that prodded my rear while the bus growled in agony up the dusty track to Karies, the Athos 'capital'. It was a place of medieval wonkiness, without cafes, bars, tavernas or any signs of frivolity. It appeared to belong neither to Greece, nor to the present century.

The crowd moved towards an administrative citadel fed by a grand flight of stairs. In the gloom at the far end of the entrance hall, tucked under the stairs, was a glass booth with a Vent-Axia size hole and a notice in English declaring that 'only those of adequate, becoming and dignified demeanour' would be allowed to stay on Athos. I had to wait an hour for my passport and permit to be re-vetted before the monk in the booth sanctioned my *diamonitirion*.

I fell into step with two pilgrims, Gregorios and Gregorios. They showed me a map and pointed to Iviron, a monastery that loomed in the distance along a gravelled track. As we walked, they rubbed their fingers together under their noses and sniffed the air like the old 'Ah Bisto' gravy ads, intended to convey how sweet and clean they found the Athos air after their polluted Athenian homes. They also told me a joke, in Greek, about the president, but I only understood two gestures – one, a pair of hands describing a shapely young woman with highly placed breasts; the other an index finger curled limply towards the stony track below.

Gregorios and Gregorios also talked about the Virgin, again relying on their hands to show, I assumed, that she was very tall. It took us an hour to reach Iviron, a hulk as impregnable as the Tower of London. The place was packed with strolling, chanting, resting and snoring pilgrims. The G Gs led me to a shaded patch of grass behind the church, in the middle of the main courtyard, where we shared olives (theirs) and sardines (mine), the latter given to me by the agent who had supplied the permit, warning me that 'meals in the monasteries are very limited'.

As the day slowly cooled, Iviron became transformed into a theatre of fundamentalist fervour. From the dark interior of the church, lit only by candles and oil lamps, came a deep rumbling of prayers and chanting. Bewildering processions of monks, some wearing the ornate robes of abbots and other senior ranks, paraded the monastery's treasures in front of the overwhelmed multitude. One silver casket, studded with jewels, was supposed to contain the shrivelled forearm of a saint.

Only later was I to learn that my 'tall Virgin' referred not to her stature, or even a statue, but the Assumption, the holiest day of the year for the monks on Mount Athos, and particularly those at Iviron where, according to legend, the Virgin was blown ashore by a storm on her way to Cyprus. Since the monks live according to the Julian calendar, Assumption was being celebrated two weeks earlier than the rest of the Christian world. This explained the crowds.

The monasteries on Mount Athos stand at the very core of the Greek Orthodox church – although you would never have guessed from the loutish moments before supper. In their rush to eat, the 200 or so pilgrims cut a procession of monks clean in two on their way between chapel and refectory. The heaviest monk used his belly as a wedge into the mob to make room for his brothers.

Once at the trough, beneath walls obscured by icons, we ate in utter silence. One monk stood on a tiny balcony above the long marble tables, reading from the scriptures, while we enjoyed a feast of little: a bowl of pasta flavoured with specks of chopped squid, bread, a glass of retsina and watermelon whose pips, when spat upon the pewter plates, sounded like heavy rain.

Since Iviron was unusually crowded because of Assumption, I could not find an empty bed. Worse still, there were no blankets, leaving me no option but to sin. I 'borrowed' one from a bed that had three, then spent a restless night on the floor of a corridor as long as a football pitch, illuminated by a pair of kerosene lamps at either end. Apart from general discomfort, I was constantly disturbed by the creak of old pilgrims treading the boards as they shuffled their way to and from the lavatory. And the bells which summoned crooked, silhouetted shadows of monks to prayer at unpredictable moments. A latch being opened at the end of the corridor resounded like a musket shot.

The monks' morning began at 3am. I got up to avoid being trampled on. I couldn't face the lavatories because the stench was overpowering. I decided to leave, to go to another monastery, setting off at first light while the August morning was still cool, following a footpath for an hour or so to the neighbouring monastery of Stavronikita. As soon as I reached the gatehouse, a monk, young but prematurely crooked, came out bearing a silver tray with a glass of water and a piece of Turkish delight, served on a dolly's tea plate. He invited me to rest under an arbour of vines.

Stavronikita, smaller than Iviron though just as impregnable, felt like a calm refuge after the fervour of the previous day. I proffered my *diamonitrion* to the monk, who spoke little English. 'Eez difficult,' he said. 'Many people.'

I worried that my demeanour, after a night on the floor, was not at its most 'adequate, becoming and dignified'. The monk kept shaking his head. I must have looked mighty weary, because he then beckoned and led me to a small room with three pairs of bunk beds tightly arranged around a wood-burning stove. I was allowed to stay for two nights.

The quiet sea lay 200 feet below, a sheer drop. The only sounds came from the breeze and the occasional bee that buzzed in through the open window. Beyond a squadron of swallows, I could see far along the coast, the faint outline of Iviron almost lost in the haze. There was no sign of a road, hotel, taverna, apartment block, shop or tent. It was Greece without jetskis, sunbeds or sunbathers, banana riders or parasols. Or people. It was as though the travel industry had never been born.

24

THE BIG CHOP

From mid-May, in the far north Norwegian port of Kirkenes, the sun stops setting. In the middle of the night, it bounces briefly on the horizon and then gets straight on with the business of dawn. The long dark Arctic winter, when temperatures can sometimes dip to fifty below, is officially over. However, word does not always get around to the elements. I went hoping for spring but, despite the long days, found snow still thick on the ground, the thermometer outside Amundsen's the grocer was showing zero and the wind was howling.

The Russian border was just a five-minute bus ride down the road. I could have booked a day trip to Murmansk through the local travel agent. But there was another reason why I had come to such a bleak global outpost. To go on a cruise, of course.

Kirkenes is the last port of call for the ships of the 'Hurtigruten', which sail the length of Norway's magnificent fish-bone of a coastline. Every day of the year, whatever the weather, one of the fleet of eleven ships leaves the base port of Bergen on a 1,300-mile round trip, stopping at the same set of thirty-four communities, some on the way up, some on the way down. The service operates as much like a bus as a boat, except that the ships run to an exact timetable – and you never get two turning up at the same time.

The route was born in 1893 when the *Vesteraalen*, a Captain Richard at the helm, first established a lifeline for the tiny fishing harbours severed from the rest of the world by the wild geography. From its very beginning, the Hurtigruten, which means the 'Fast Route', was also a tourist draw. One of the earliest brochures extolled the natural pleasures of Europe's least developed, most dramatic coastline.

Those early descriptions are every bit as true today as they were a century ago – but for one essential difference. With the arrival of both airstrips and roads – including Euroroute 6, which leads all the way from Rome to Kirkenes – the sea is no longer the only approach. But it is still the most scenic and by far the most romantic.

The carriage of cargo, anything from coffins to cod, as well as locals, still makes the Hurtigruten distinctly different from a conventional cruise. There is no choice of itinerary, for example, since each of the eleven ships sails an identical eleven-day itinerary, although you can book shorter sectors. But which ship you choose is another matter.

I sailed on the *Harald Jarl*, the oldest of the fleet, which was celebrating its fortieth birthday during my voyage. Aside from the war years, she has sailed up and down the same coastline ever since her maiden voyage. Her engine had enough on the clock to have circumnavigated the globe 126 times.

As tourists have become more commercially important than other cargo, so the newer members of the Hurtigruten fleet have been built to compete with conventional cruise ships. They have swimming pools and panoramic lounges, a choice of restaurants and en-suite cabins. On *Harald Jarl* there were more bunks than beds, half the cabins had to share washrooms and there were two sittings in the one tiny dining room. If you want a holiday, pick a new ship. But I was after a voyage, one with a real sense of time and place.

Harald Jarl was old, but no rust tub. She was a lovingly preserved piece of maritime history, all brass, bells, hooters and woods. Yet, by the time you read these words, this icon of Norway's merchant marine will be on the scrap heap, existing only in the history books. Or so I had assumed.

The pending death sentence on poor *Harald* had nothing to do with her ability to perform as a seaworthy vessel but everything to do with the changing economics of the industry. Weighing in at just over 2,000 tons, the same mark on the scales as an Isle of Wight ferry, she carried fewer than a third as many passengers as her far bigger sisters. Although still making a profit for her owners, her siblings were making more.

'The *Harald Jarl* is a proper ship,' maintained her forty-one-year-old skipper Jon Olaf Klodiussen, who embodied the company tradition of assigning its youngest captain to its oldest ship. I asked him what she was like to drive. 'If you can sail *Harald Jarl* you can sail any ship in the world. She is like a classroom, with just one propeller, not thrusters here and there and everywhere. On new ships, the captain sits in a box and plays with machines. Here I open the door and put my nose into the weather. I sail by the nature, not the computer.'

In Kirkenes, nature was punching us right on the nose. Faced with the full force of a cruel polar wind screaming in unopposed from the North Pole, *Harald* was already gently swaying while still tethered to the quay. An hour after casting off, heading into the teeth of the wind, Rita Salberg, the ship's 'courier', announced on the speaker that it might be a good idea if we all sat down. 'We have a little movement at the moment.'

The passage around the North Cape, Europe's 'Tierra del Fuego', leapt right out of the pages of a sea dog's yarn. I took one look at my supper of baked trout and decided to flee to my bunk, curling under the duvet and falling asleep in my rocking and rolling cradle to the soft thump of the engine and the ocean pounding on my porthole.

Several hours later I was woken by the sound of the anchor chain cascading over the side. We had rounded the Cape, the sea had calmed, the sun beamed in through my porthole and I was hungry. I even managed a couple of seagulls' eggs, a sure sign of a settled stomach. I ventured on deck and watched the crew open up the cargo hatches while the deck crane swung into action. A fork-lift scurried along the quay like a demented cockroach ready to offload the goods.

Days soon began to have a pattern. No matter the time, there were always passengers on deck watching the harbour action. Usually there was time for a stroll, for a potter around the pretty pale blue, ochre, oxblood and army-green houses, and for a lady travelling with her Rottweiler to take it off for a pee. There were even a few optional excursions but, unlike a cruise ship, the ports were there for a purpose rather than a pleasure.

We called at Hammerfest, the world's most northerly town, on the same latitude as Siberia, and Honningsvag, the world's most northerly village with the world's most northerly strawberry fields. Then there was Tromso, the 'Paris of the North', its approaches still guarded by the 'Adolf Gun' which could fire 42cm shells.

I spent a lot of the twenty-four-hour Arctic light leaning over the rails, awed by the passing scenery, watching seabirds pirouette in our wake. The landscapes grew more spectacular by the mile, from the treeless, bushless, monochrome North Cape plateau to a coast of islands and soaring peaks. *Harald Jarl* weaved a course between them and nosed into narrow, will-she-won't-she-fit fjords. We had to skip one particularly skinny one because, as Rita Salberg announced, there was a risk of an avalanche hitting the decks.

The *Harald Jarl* continued to the turnaround town of Bergen but I jumped ship when we reached the Lofoten Islands, an archipelago of immense, awesome grandeur lapped by Caribbean clear waters. In winter, the islands are the richest fish larder in the world, the cod arriving from the Arctic to spawn in waters warmed by the Gulf Stream, where they are scooped up by hundreds of fishing boats. In summer the place leads a seasonal retirement, the cod spoils left to dry on high wooden racks, swaying in the breeze like grey undies on washing lines, before being shipped abroad, the bodies to Italy and the heads to Nigeria.

This body and head returned to the UK where, some twenty years later, I decided to check on the fate of the *Harald Jarl*. Far from heading for a ship's graveyard, she had been bought, fully renovated and upgraded as a proper cruise ship, even venturing as far as Antarctica. She was renamed *Andrea* by one owner, who subsequently ran into financial difficulties and the ship was impounded in Split. A new owner paid off the debt and renamed her *Serenissima*, and the reincarnated *Harald Jarl* simply carried on cruising.

25

ROUND THE BEND

I first went to Texas in London. In St James's, in an alleyway next to Berry Bros & Rudd the wine merchant, there's a plaque marking the site of the 'Embassy of the Republic of Texas'. It opened in 1836, when Texas became an independent country. In 1845 the state joined the Union and the embassy abruptly closed, leaving £160 in unpaid rent.

A few days later I flew to Austin, the state capital, not to collect the debt but a car from Hertz. The agent handed over the keys with an ear-to-ear smile. 'Y'all have a big time now, you hear,' she added. Smiles, and times, are big in Texas, just like everything else. Fifteen lesser American states could all fit inside its boundaries, and so would several European countries. Even 20:20 visionaries need to squint to bring far horizons into focus.

My prime destination was the Big Bend National Park, a 475-mile drive from Austin. But before setting off, I went batting. By a curious irony, the state's most extraordinary wildlife phenomena takes place in the very heart of the city.

Every sunset, up to a million bats rise from their roosts in the concrete expansion cracks of the Congress Avenue Bridge which spans the Colorado River. They swarm like an Aladdin's genie in an undulating cloud, silhouetted against the setting sun. They are off on their nightly noshing on more than 20,000 pounds of insects.

The best ringside seat for the spectacle is the lawn of the Hyatt hotel, beer in hand, secure in the knowledge that this is probably the only time and place in the world where, with such an army of predators on the hunt, no mosquito would ever contemplate a supper of human blood.

Bats aside, Austin is a perfect gateway for a trip to the Big Bend. Passing first through the pretty limestone 'Hill Country', of grazing longhorn cattle, dude ranches, juniper and oak forests, carpets of bluebonnets and nodding donkeys guzzling up oil, my first stop was for a sausage at the 'Little Germany' colony of Fredericksburg. A few miles on, just outside the aptly named town of Junction, I joined Interstate I-10, the highway that reaches all the way from Florida to California.

As the day expanded, so the cars thinned to the frequency of a dripping tap and the tarmac became the dining table for turkey vultures pecking away on roadkill. Further west, the scenery balded to a khaki wasteland of yucca, cactus and assorted scrub, with the occasional 'Don't Mess with Texas' billboard, the state's upfront way of requesting people not to drop litter.

I approached Big Bend through the back door, via the ghost town of Shafter, scene of the last Native American uprising, and the border town of Presidio. I then headed east, following the green banks of the Rio Grande, the rocky ridges of Mexico surfacing on the far bank. I stopped at the riverside town on Lajitas which once elected a beer-swilling goat as its mayor.

Big Bend is the remote, empty, dead end of America. According to Apache legend, when the Great Spirit made the rest of the world and had put all the birds in the sky, the stars in the heavens and the fish in the sea, he dumped the leftovers right here, turning a deep U-bend of the Rio Grande into a giant skip of mixed hardcore.

The National Park, covering 1,250 square miles, bigger than the whole of Lancashire, is one of America's largest but least known, with just 350,000 visitors a year compared with the Grand Canyon's 6.3 million. They're a mix of motorists, hikers, bikers and motor-campers, one of which I saw towing a car at its rear, a set of mountain bikes lashed to the front, a couple of canoes on the roof and a sign which read, 'He who dies with the most toys, wins.' Very Texan.

I stopped at the National Park Visitor Center to collect a map and a few 'safety tips on how to avoid encounters with rattlesnakes, mountain lion and flash floods'. The park is full of everything that bites, from mosquitoes (we're well out of range of their massacre at Austin) to each of America's four poisonous snakes, tarantulas, horseflies and distinctly uncuddly bears. My only encounter with nasty nature was from a cactus whose dagger spikes met my be-shorted shins. Most at risk are horse riders; a fall would be like skydiving onto a bed of nails.

All but a tiny fragment of Big Bend belongs to the Chihuahua desert, the thirstiest landscape imaginable. The summer mercury here can shoot right off the top of the tube. Bang in the middle stand the Chisos Mountains, where I touched a 400 million-year-old rock with one hand and the petals of a day-old flower with the other.

In parts, you can almost reach out and touch Mexico, which is a concept far more elusive for many Mexicans hoping to go the other way. At Boquillas del Carmen – the mouthpiece of Carmen – I took a one-man-and-an-oar ferry across the river, followed by a ride in the back of a mechanically challenged pick-up to a Mexican hamlet snoring in the afternoon heat, *mariachi* music crackling from a tinny radio in a fly-blown bar.

Back in the US, I spent a night in in a town called Marathon, checking into the mission-style Cage Hotel, built ninety years ago by a pioneer Texas rancher called Alfred Gage. My room had a saddle, branding iron and a pair of chaps on the wall, horseshoe on the door, an Indian blanket on the bed, and the hide of something on the floor.

My other urban bookend, or point three of my Texan triangle, was San Antonio. The cheapest way to get there would have been to enlist, since all recruits to the US Air Force come here for their initial training. With five bases, it is the town's biggest industry. Tourism runs a close second, particular for American visitors who come for the Tex Mex cultural mix and the Alamo.

Remember the Alamo? Well, maybe not if you're a Brit, but it is a sacred site, especially to born and raised Texans who even take off their whopper, ten-gallon Stetsons when entering, something they are loathed to do even when eating. Or dancing. One of a chain of old Spanish missions, the Alamo is where, in 1836, Colonel Travis, Davy Crockett and 200 patriots battled to their death in the struggle for Texan independence from Mexico.

Which, in a roundabout sort of way, take us right back to St James.

26

EAR MARKED

One winter, in the late seventies, I rented a poky, first-floor bedsit in the dreary fringes to the west of New York's arty SoHo neighbourhood.

It was little more than a kitchen with a bed and a bath. On the ground floor was a 'Chinese Egg Factory', according to the sign over the permanently shuttered shop front. In the two months I lived there, I saw neither eggs, chickens or Chinamen.

Right across the street, but unknown to me when I first saw the room and agreed on the sublet, was a depot for the city's refuse trucks. Every morning at 5am I would be woken by the cacophonous roar of engines firing up for their morning rounds.

Although the location was seriously underwhelming, there was a wonderful bonus. Just around the corner stood a bar called the EAR. It wasn't one of those heavy drinking joints that you often come across in grim parts of US cities, sadly patronised by lonely drinkers, but a real 'local'.

The reason for the unusual name was not the result of cool branding, but simply because the cheapest neon sign the owner could afford was a bog-standard one with 'BAR' written in red neon. Just to make his place less impersonal, he had blacked out the two 'bellies' of the letter 'B', leaving an 'E', hence the EAR. Clever.

Every patch of wall space at the EAR was covered in photos, paintings, potty artefact, even an ancient, green metallic, 'West Croydon' British Rail station sign. They played great music. There was a counter where sports fans sat on bar stools watching basketball, baseball or NFL football, and a back room with a handful of tables, where they served a few good, affordable dishes. The tables had paper cloths and jars of crayons so diners could doodle.

I used to eat there a couple of times a week. One night I was with friends and we spotted David Hockney with a couple of pals on a nearby table. While waiting for their food to arrive, Hockney drew things on his paper cloth. As it was still relatively early in his path of fame, I wasn't sure if anyone else had recognised him so, after he and his pals had finished eating and were getting ready to leave, I thought I might casually saunter over and scoop up his creation. But, at the precise moment they rose from their chairs, a waiter rushed over, whipped off the paper and disappeared into the kitchen. It was probably the most valuable tip ever.

The main reason for my being in New York at the time, odd though it may sound, was to translate a book on growing vegetables, newly published in the UK, into 'American' so that it could be sold on the US market. I'll explain my veg credentials later, but I had accepted the job partly because I relished the opportunity to go back to New York, a city I loved.

Most days I took the subway uptown to work in the library of the New York Horticultural Society. The four friendly, green-fingered staffers made me very welcome, set me up with a desk and were always helpful when I got stuck with US names for some obscure fruit or vegetable.

One day, just prior to the Society closing its doors for New Year, three peculiar things happened. The first was the arrival of a woman who worked at the Prospect Park Zoo in Brooklyn. 'We have,' she explained to the librarians, 'a problem. We have a 300-ton heap of animal manure that we just don't know what to do with. Do you think that any of your members might like to come to the zoo and just help themselves? There's hippo, rhino and even a little llama in the mix. The compost value should be really good.'

A second person arrived mid-morning, a member of a new radical group called the Green Guerillas. She thought, hoped, that the Society would be interested in helping promote a new city-wide project. 'We're planning to fill a lot of balloons with water and mixes of wild seeds and lob them, over the fences, into vacant lots all over the city. With luck,' she continued, 'the seeds will germinate and turn these terrible blights on the city streets into attractive gardens.'

That same day one of the team at the Society also mentioned a newly launched scheme called 'Operation Green Thumb'. Community groups committed to improving the look of their local hood would be able to lease vacant city-owned lots for the princely sum of a dollar a year if they made a commitment to turning them into attractive, natural spaces. The Department of Sanitation – my noisy neighbours – had even agreed to take away any garbage prior to planting.

A word now about my own green credentials. I was, at that time, a gardening journalist, writing exclusively about growing fruit and vegetables. My focus was on how those living in towns without the luxury of a large garden, or even any garden at all, could at least attempt a modicum of self-sufficiency. It was quite a hot topic at the time but most practitioners, and writers on the subject, were living on smallholdings in the countryside. My 'urban farming' idea caught on and I wrote a book that Doubleday published in the USA. *The New York Times* also commissioned me to write a few features, on subjects that ranged from raising strawberries in pots on your balcony to growing mushrooms under your bed.

Hearing about these fascinating community happenings, I thought I might be able to interest the *NYT* in a story. I called the Home section to speak to the gardening editor, my regular contact, but she was not at her desk. Without my asking, I was put through to the editor in charge of the whole Home section, a woman I had never spoken to, let alone met.

I was nervous but pressed on with my proposal. She listened but didn't say a word. I even thought, for one moment, that she'd hung up. When I'd finished my pitch I muttered, erred and aahed, and waited. After a long silence she abruptly snapped, 'I like it. Your scoop. Copy by tomorrow night, please. 1,200 words.'

My joy was soon followed by panic. I found out more about the poo, the balloons and Operation Green Thumb, and then went back to my Egg Factory to write the story. After various failed attempts and rewrites, typing away on the kitchen breakfast bar (actually a shelf), going through a full bottle of Tippex (this was still typewriter days), taking a final draft to read in the EAR, then waking up in the night to write it all over again, I finished the piece at the same time that the refuse trucks ignited.

I called the *NYT* and they sent a courier to collect the article. It was New Year's Eve. A time to celebrate – guess where? – at the EAR. And, of course, again the following Saturday when the piece appeared as the front-page story in Home. I was thrilled.

I now take a giant leap in time. In April 2015, I was invited to review a new super-hip New York hotel, the Hugo. I looked up the address. Coincidentally, it was just around the corner from the EAR, yards from the Chinese Egg Factory and the refuse truck depot. Except that the Egg Factory was no more, the building bearing tell-tale signs of restoration. And not only had the trucks vanished but the lot where they had once roared into life at ungodly hours had been implanted with an office block.

Thankfully, the EAR was still there, the interior just as I remembered, the wall décor unchanged. I asked for a table, next to the Hockney one, ordered a beer and a burger and looked around. Even in this dynamic, ever-reincarnating city, some things – thankfully – never change.

27

WORLD IN CRISIS

On that devastating, deadly day, September 11th 2001, I was in the USA, in Boston, staying in a hotel on Charles Street. I'd had breakfast and was waiting in the lobby for a guide from the tourist office to show me the city's highlights.

She arrived, some twenty minutes late. She apologised for the delay, explaining how the traffic had been far heavier than usual and that she had heard, on her car radio, that a plane had crashed into the World Trade Centre in New York.

We both assumed it was most likely a small private plane, a Cesna or similar, a dramatic, awful accident of which we would, no doubt, be hearing more. We set off on foot from the hotel.

After a couple of hundred yards, we spotted a crowd of people gathered round a shop window. Wondering what could be so riveting, we stood at the back and peered over their heads. The store was a TV showroom. All the sets were showing the same images, of the Twin Towers, one of which was billowing an enormous cumulonimbus of smoke.

The crowd was silent. As we watched, a plane, a big commercial airline, flew straight into the second tower, exploding in an immense fireball. The crowd let out a mass chorus of groans and screams, punctuated by cries of 'Oh my God' and other expletives. The scene was horrifying.

We drifted away from the crowd and my guide asked what I wanted to do. I thought it more important that she should decide what she wanted to do. Would I mind, she asked, if she were to go back home to her family? 'If I lived in Boston,' I reassured her, 'I would want to do exactly the same.' As it transpired, my own home in London, and my family, was definitely not an option for me, as all outbound flights were cancelled, incoming flights diverted and Boston's Logan airport closed.

Downtown Boston began to evacuate. Workers in the Hancock Building, the tallest in the city, were pouring out of the entrance and heading off in all directions. Shopkeepers were locking up and closing shutters. I saw an elderly gent, wearing old army combat fatigues, purposefully pacing the pavement, braced for action but still wearing his slippers.

The roads were jammed. Two cars, clearly in a rush, collided. The drivers, a man and a woman, stepped out of their vehicles, checked the damage and angrily approached one another. The man shrugged and said, 'Let's just blame it on the day,' and the pair shook hands, gave each other God's blessing, got back into their freshly dented cars and drove off.

In no time at all, Boston became a ghost town. The roads emptied and people simply vanished. Back in my hotel room, I tried calling home but couldn't get a line (this was in pre-mobile days; well, mine anyway). I put on the TV and watched the news unfold, including details of the two other aircraft attacks. I felt totally numb, homesick and strangely rooted to the spot, unable to decide what to do next.

The original plan had been to meet up with fellow journalist Peter Hughes, to test drive a new walking itinerary in Maine arranged by a company called Inntravel. Peter had been due to fly into Boston that very day, but that was clearly not going to happen. The country was now in complete lockdown and braced for what felt like the start of a terrifying global conflict. I later found out that his flight had been diverted to Halifax, Nova Scotia, along with scores of other inbound aircraft, and Peter had been billeted in a camp set up by the Red Cross. Locals brought the passengers fresh peaches and let them use their phones.

I finally managed to call home, to reassure my wife that I was OK, but at the time I felt that nothing was ever going to be the same again. I also got a call from my friend Kathy, who lived in one of the suburbs of Boston. She had been planning to come into the city that evening for dinner. She called to cancel, hugely apologetic but saying she really wanted to stay at home and just be with her family. Of course I understood. I wanted to be home with mine.

I'd just switched on the TV, to one of the news channels, when the hotel phone rang. It was the news editor of the newspaper I worked for, asking if I could help with its coverage of events as they were unable to get any of their reporters to Boston. He explained how the city was emerging as a 'crucible in the plot' since some of the hijackers had boarded two of the planes used in the attack at Logan airport. 'So, David,' he proposed, 'what I need you to do is go out to the airport and find out as much info as you can about those guys. Interview anybody who might have spoken to them, at the check-in counter, the car rental agents, maybe the coffee shop.' I agreed to help, hung up the phone and wondered whether I'd even be able get out to Logan, given the shutdown and the super-heightened security, let alone meet anyone.

I called Logan, managed to get through to someone in the press office and asked if I would be able to access the airport despite the likely barriers. I must have sounded more legitimate than I felt and was told my name would be left with the soldiers manning the newly installed barricades, and to ask for the media centre on arrival.

With one eye and both ears on the TV, I started to gather a few items – notebook, pens, laptop, passport, etc. I was just about to leave the room when the news presenter announced that there was shortly to be an 'important press briefing at Logan'. I doubted, even if I managed to grab a taxi, whether I'd make it in time, but I decided to give it a go.

While I was pondering what to do, the presenter announced that the briefing was going to be screened live and in full. I stayed in my room, lay on the bed with my laptop on my knees, watched the broadcast, took notes and sent the details back to London, knowing that there was little chance of anyone getting anything more 'scoopy' from a first-hand visit to the airport.

The briefing was interesting, not that it revealed any more detail about the hijackers, but it transpired that the authorities at Logan had, over recent months, issued scores of security passes that they could no longer account for. I dutifully emailed this recent revelation and felt 'job done'.

The rest of my days in the US, waiting for the airports to reopen and the skies to return to flying duties, were rather strange and other-worldly. I took a bus to Maine and spent a few days walking the route that Peter and I had planned to follow. I then took a train to New York (my original plan – and airline ticket – had always been to return to the UK from JFK airport). Approaching the city, I could still see a thick plume of smoke rising from the skeletal remains of the towers.

I had a room booked at the downtown W Hotel, whose entire lobby and lounge area were filled with exhausted, grimy, silent and emotionally drained rescue workers draped over sofas and lying on the floor. I think I was the only 'proper' guest.

I managed to get on the first available flight back to the UK. Assuming there would be almost impenetrable security hurdles to navigate, I reached JFK four hours ahead of the scheduled departure. Everything was very quiet, almost strangely relaxed. There were no more hurdles than the usual checks. Airside of the security gates I saw four armed soldiers casually standing around, munching burgers. I sat in front of a TV screen, watching an 'aviation expert' on CNN News tell the interviewer that 'the last thing in the world I would do right now was get on a plane'. Mine was three quarters empty.

A PS

On a much more recent visit to New York I went to the 9/11 Memorial Museum. I tried to comprehend the huge loss of life, the force that could do so much human and physical damage, all those buckled, twisted, contorted metal structures, the pretzel twist of girders, a fire engine broken like a child's toy...

Even more upsetting were the voices of those contacting loved ones, especially the flight attendant on board one of the hijacked aircraft. She was recorded leaving a message on the answerphone for her husband, saying goodbye and almost managing to say 'I love you' but breaking into sobs before a colossal explosion.

Photographs of firemen walking up stairways to their deaths, while others were walking down to their lives, were equally poignant, as were images of the falling bodies. One photographer had captured a woman adjusting her skirt for modesty before leaping to her death.

It's the most disturbing museum I've ever visited, the impact no doubt heightened by how close I had been on the day.

I was brought sharply back to reality on leaving the museum when I muttered a goodbye to one of the security guards. He hoped I had 'enjoyed' the museum. 'It certainly gives you a lot of bang for your buck.'

28

RONNIE IN RIO

Ask most people to name famous Brazilians and the late Great Train Robber Ronnie Biggs could well figure in the list along with the likes of Pele, Ayrton Senna, Jair Bolsonaro and 'Brazilian Bombshell' Carmen Miranda.

In 1997 I arranged to interview Biggs at his home in Rio de Janeiro. Having successfully managed to establish himself as one of the city's main visitor attractions, I wanted to talk to him not about train heists but tourism.

I called him from my Rio hotel soon after checking in. 'Come on over,' said Biggs. 'I've hurt my knee, so let yourself in through the gate and down the stairs. I've got a big dog but he is well fed. Just let him smell you. He's called Blitz. Like a bombing raid.'

Biggs had been living in Rio for the past twenty-seven years, the last few in the old hillside district of Santa Teresa which, despite whatever proceeds he may or may not have retained from the robbery, had none of the glamour of Ipanema or

Copacabana. Nowadays, it's become rather fashionable but in the seventies the neighbourhood was threatening, especially at night. Hence Blitz, the bear-sized Rottweiler.

Soon after nightfall, I took a taxi to the house, opened the gate as instructed and braced myself as Blitz bounded up the path, growling, barking and unbelievably terrifying. I offered the back of my hand and held my breath, but thankfully I passed the fragrance test. Blitz followed me down the path to the front door, which was ajar. I called out and was summoned inside.

Biggs, author of two books on the robbery (one about the crew who got away) and a set of lyrics on a Sex Pistols album, was earning a decent living from tourism. 'I call it the Ronnie Biggs Experience,' he told me. Small groups of visitors, mainly Brits, could arrange to come to his house for dinner, for around £40 a head (twice as much by today's prices), 'which includes plenty of grub and all the drinks. I then tell a few stories. I'm a bit like an old Agatha Christie script. There's no limit to the number of times you can tell the same tale'.

If you weren't aware of the Biggs back story, you would put the man squarely in the good-bloke, diamond-geezer category, with a wealth of good craic to share, both about life in Rio as well as the robbery and its aftermath. 'I usually finish with the Filth's disastrous attempt at trying to kidnap me.'

At home, sitting with his big mug of tea, his knee stitched, pinned and bandaged after a recent fall over a low-lying chain fence, crutches to one side, Biggs appeared much mellowed by time. He was no Blitz; more Labrador or golden retriever. But a change in the extradition laws between Britain and Brazil had put a big question mark over his future, which was was clearly worrying him.

If, (and as we now know, when), the UK authorities, still hellbent on revenge after Biggs had eluded them for more than three decades, managed to haul him back, those Biggs house parties would be deleted from the Rio visitor menu.

One Brazilian tourist official had tried to reassure him: 'We will never let you go. You are one of our number-one tourist attractions.'

As I was about to take my leave of both Biggs and Blitz, the latter now asleep with his head on my feet (I contemplated leaving my shoes behind rather than risk disturbing him), the phone rang. It was, Biggs explained, a croupier calling from a cruise ship, still somewhere at sea but planning to bring a group of admirers to the house. After noting the date, time and numbers, Biggs hung up the phone and a mischievous smile crept across the face of the old villain. 'She said that most of them were dancers,' he said. 'Sounds interesting.'

29

ODD VIBRATIONS

Of all the islands in the world, none quite kindles dreams of paradise as those of the South Seas, that barely detectable scatter of confetti in the biggest, emptiest, least explored ocean on the planet. This is a tale of just one of them, and specifically, the island's only resort. It will, hopefully, have undergone a whole raft of changes since my visit more than two decades ago, but just in case it hasn't, it had better remain nameless.

The flight to Fiji, via Los Angeles, was long and exhausting but alleviated by two things. One, getting an upgrade. And two, sitting next to Judith Chalmers, a doyenne of travel writers, the industry's equivalent to royalty and one of the nicest people in the business. I had met Judith on a few previous occasions and we chatted on the flight. She was travelling with a film crew from the ITV travel programme *Wish You Were Here*. On arrival she travelled to one island, I to another.

The final leg of my journey was a hop aboard a moth-size

seaplane with a shoeless pilot, the very last stage being a knee-deep wade ashore, stepping from the pontoon into the opal calm of a gorgeous lagoon. A porter carried my bag on his head.

I was greeted on the beach by a huge man wearing a skirt and a hibiscus tucked behind his ear, who offered me a welcome drink in a coconut shell. Another member of staff strummed a ukulele under a palm tree. After being shown to my romantic, frond-thatched *bure*, I went for a swim, took a walk to the island's highest spot to admire the view and generally padded around the resort with no fixed agenda.

At 7pm the twenty or so guests, all couples apart from me, gathered for drinks on the beach before sitting down for dinner at a long, communal table.

I felt as though I'd gate-crashed a private party. Everyone seemed to know everyone else, although most had only met since arriving on the island. I sat next to an Australian who told me, turning aside from his wife, how he really loved to party, big time. 'As you will know, David,' he added, 'there's only so many times you can strangle a duck.'

After the main course, the manager stood up and asked us to give the chef a round of applause, 'for the excellent dinner we have all been enjoying'. She then turned to me. 'Now,' she said, 'it's your turn, David. As our new arrival, maybe you'd just like to stand up and let us all share your initial impressions of our island paradise.'

A cheer went up and a round of applause. I managed to mumble my way through a few choice words of praise and quickly sat down. I got another round of applause, although far more muted than the one for the chef or even my introduction from the manager.

After dessert, the couples gradually peeled away from the table and drifted off back to their *bures*. I wandered back to mine, walking through the warm night air orchestrated by a choir of cicadas. The room had been illuminated by a pair of lanterns, the bed turned down for the night. I undressed, blew out the candles and got into bed.

I felt something rather hard under the sheet, like a short, smooth stick. I lifted it out and fumbled with it in the darkness, trying to fathom out what it was. I accidentally pressed a button on the side, which kick-started a motor. It was a vibrator.

Aside from the shock of finding it, and realising what it was, I worried that the sound of the motor would carry far in the still evening air and that some, probably several, neighbours would be smirking, knowing that someone, somewhere, maybe that bloke travelling on his own, was pleasuring someone, or himself, before going to sleep. I turned it off as quickly as I could.

At breakfast the next morning I felt a little sheepish but nobody gave me any funny looks. I sat opposite an English couple whom I'd met the night before. They did ask whether I'd had a good night's sleep but their expressions didn't suggest a hidden agenda.

I had, in fact, been woken far too early as two men had started hammering and banging soon after first light, working on the construction of a small kiosk just across from my *bure*. I told the English couple. The man, Paul, sympathised and said that it was a shame that the manager hadn't put me in one of the *bures* at the other end of the resort, where he and his wife were billeted. 'It's so quiet there,' he added, 'you wouldn't even hear the guests next door no matter what they got up to.'

I agreed it was a shame. 'I know,' said my new friend, turning to his wife. 'Carol, why don't you take David along to our *bure* so that he can see it for himself?'

Carol stood up with a smile. 'Of course, David. Shall we go now? We can come back for more coffee afterwards.'

Carol and I left the communal breakfast table and walked along the beach towards the other *bures*. She took my arm. 'We so love it here,' she told me, giving me a friendly squeeze. 'I can't bear the thought of ever going home.' We reached the steps to the deck of her *bure* and went inside. 'Here we are. And here's the bedroom,' she announced.

I walked into the room ahead of Carol, saw the bed, a four-poster with muslin draped around the sides. My eyes shot straight to a pair of handcuffs that hung from the top of one of the posts. Everything told me to turn away, to take my eyes off the bloody handcuffs, but they stayed riveted. 'Lovely bedroom, isn't it, David?' said Carol.

'Oh yes, lovely.' I managed to look away from the handcuffs, glanced around the room and quickly turned towards the door. 'Fabulous room, yes, and yes, so quiet. Just like you said. Shall we go and get that coffee now?'

I was only staying on the island for one night. My seaplane arrived mid-morning and the pilot stood in the water holding the plane's pontoon.

Just as I was about to wade out, Paul and Carol came scampering down the beach wearing the skimpiest of swimwear and plastered in sun cream. 'We must have our photo taken with you,' they said. 'Stand in the middle, between the two of us, and put your arms around us.' I did as I was told, my hands slithering round their oily waists, then bade them and the manager farewell. Maybe it was my imagination, fuelled by the confrontation with what were rather mild items of erotica, and probably all the more startling since I was travelling solo, but I felt relieved to be leaving.

There is a postscript to this particular story. By coincidence, a week or so later, I again crossed paths with the ITV film crew on another island. I first bumped into the director, Mark, a lively young lad who was fascinated by my tales of 'love island', one they were not down to visit. He offered a word of caution. 'Whatever you do, don't mention the vibrator or the handcuffs to Judith. She's a very proper lady, as you know. She'll never believe you. Nor will she find the story the least bit amusing.'

Ten minutes later Judith wandered over and seemed really pleased to meet up again. But the warmth behind her greeting was not to last. Mark, the rogue, turned to Judith and, with a cheeky smile, said, 'Hey, Judith, you'll never guess what David came across on his last island. He was given a vibrator to play with in his bed and a couple of guests invited him to take part in a bondage threesome, handcuffs provided.'

Judith gave me a cold stare. 'David, you should not make up things like that. That's an outrageous thing to say. I'm very surprised at you.'

30

GOING TO A BALL

In 2011, to celebrate New Zealand having been chosen to host the next World Cup Rugby tournament, I was invited by the tourist board in London to a reception – inside a rugby ball.

The 'ball' was a giant, fully-enclosed marquee, shaped like a rugby ball, capable of holding around sixty people. It had first been seen positioned below the Eiffel Tower in 2007, prior to France staging the tournament. It had been transported to London and erected, or probably inflated, on the South Bank, close to Tower Bridge. Inside, by some clever cinematic technology, images of the All Blacks in action were being screened, the experience not unlike IMAX in the round. Or, in this case, in the oval.

The invitation to the event requested 'business attire', which did seem surprisingly formal for a Kiwi occasion. However, willing as I was to play the game (dress-wise, not rugby), I was unable to wear a jacket. I had recently broken my thumb playing tennis and the plaster that encased it couldn't possibly be manoeuvred into a jacket sleeve. So I wore my smartest pullover and chinos, my arm supported by a sling.

When I arrived, the ball was in full swing. I helped myself with my good hand to a bottle of New Zealand's Lion Ale from the ice bucket by the bar and was greeted by Greg Anderson, then head of the NZ's UK tourist board whom I had met on several previous occasions. 'Hi, David, glad you could come,' he greeted. 'Looks as if you've been up against the All Blacks. Hope that sling isn't too much of a hassle,' he added. 'Let me introduce you to a few people.'

I didn't catch the name of the first man I met, but he was soon asking how I'd managed to break my thumb. We small-talked about tennis, rugby and other sporty topics. A waitress approached with a tray of canapes. Appreciating that I didn't have a free hand, the man said, 'Hey, let me hold your beer while you grab something.' He took the bottle, I chose and consumed a canape, then took back the beer and we carried on chatting.

The man had a distinct Kiwi accent so I asked whether he was based in London. 'Ah no,' he replied. 'In fact I'm going back to Auckland on tonight's flight.'

I asked how long he'd been in the UK.

'Just arrived a couple of days ago.'

'Wow, and you're heading back so soon?'

'I have to. I've only just taken up my new post, so I really need to go back and get my feet under the desk.'

I knew, but hadn't given it much thought, that there had recently been a change in government in New Zealand, so I blindly pressed on.

'Which post would that be?' said I.

'Minister of Tourism,' said he.

'Oh, I see. Of course.' I was impressed, at the same time felt an idiot for not knowing, especially as I'm sure that's how Greg may well have introduced us. 'Was that a portfolio you had wanted in the new Cabinet?' said I, wading forth with, I thought, a seamless recovery.

'Very much so. In addition to being Prime Minister, I also get to look after one government department. I wanted tourism because it's such an important sector in our economy.'

The man was John Key, New Zealand's new PM.

I'm sure there can be few countries in the world with a Prime Minister that would not only chat so informally, without any PR minders to intercede let alone a heavy, wiggly wired security gorilla, but to look after the beer of a wounded nobody.

A PS

A few years later, while staying on a resort in the Maldives, I told this story to the general manager, another New Zealander and a big butch of a man. As I finished the tale, I noticed that his eyes were, ever so slightly, beginning to water. 'That story,' he said, 'makes me very proud to be a Kiwi. Very, very proud.'

31

PLAYING POLO

I can't quite believe that I once spent the best part of a day, several Februarys ago, strutting beside the canals of Venice dressed as Marco Polo. I wore flowing crimson robes, a hat shaped like a fat, circular sausage and a mass of gold frills around my shoulders. Tourists even asked me to pose for selfies.

The reason for the costume was to go to a ball, one of several staged in Venice during Carnival week. Mine was rented from a shop called Venetia, run with a flourish of high camp by Vladamir, Tomaso and Nico de Leo. After helping me into the robes they stood me in front of the mirror and discussed their latest creation.

'Alora, Marco Polo. Very, very nice.'

'Ah si, si. Those colours. Perfetto.'

'Perhaps he should be a Doge. Davide, maybe you would prefer a Doge.'

I definitely did not see myself as a Doge, especially since

Doge Wear in Venetia cost three times as much as a Polo outfit. I quickly settled on the ancient mariner, paid for the twenty-four-hour loan, wrapped him in a carrier bag and set off in search of a mask.

Everyone goes a bit bonkers in Venice during Carnival, and the best way to catch the spirit is to dress up. According to official literature, Carnival takes its origin from 'ancient proprietary rites of the sowing season and of rebirth: a fertility feast of sex, excess and dressing up,' so costumes are all part of the scene, along with masks, balls, parades, street entertainment, gala dinners, and, who knows, sex and excess.

If you simply wander the streets wearing a T-shirt and a pair of jeans, you will certainly see what Carnival in Venice is all about. But if you want to *feel* what it's all about, to really get under the skin of the occasion, you need to dress up. You should also bag a ticket to a ball, many of which are staged in the fabulously opulent *palazzi* that line the Grand Canal. Each has a strict dress code. In some, you can get away with a tuxedo – 'lo smoking' – or a fancy gown, plus an essential mask. Others demand full historic costume, hence me and Marco Polo.

Marco Polo, being somewhat of a social butterfly, went to two balls. One, organised by the local chapter of the young Rotarians to raise money for charity, was held in the fifteenth-century palazzo Vendramin dei Carmini, still being restored but nonetheless heaving with atmosphere, the courtyard illuminated entirely by candles, the interiors by chandeliers.

The other was less glamorous, held in a hotel near the railway station, but was much more affordable. The evening began with prosecco and nibbles, followed by dinner with wine (I lost count of the courses) served in a pretty dining room. Entertainment was provided by a troupe of hysterical clowns and a string quartet in period dress playing baroque music, followed by dancing. There were around a hundred guests, a mix of tourists and locals, mostly in costume, and the mood was wonderful.

There are many happenings in town besides balls. The first of the costumed parades is Feste delle Marie. Led by seven girls called Maria from each of the city's seven *sestriere* (or boroughs), they represent young girls once kidnapped by pirates, rescued by Venetians and then presented to the Doge for his pleasure. Maybe I chose the wrong costume after all.

A number of special carnival walks are also organised, with visitors being shown around by a costumed 'codega', a lantern-carrying servant who, in the Middle Ages, would lead his noble employers along the dodgy night alleyways. Rosanna, my codega, showed me the convent – now a police station – where Casanova seduced a beautiful nun and a bridge called Tette, named after the bare-breasted prostitutes who used to sit in nearby windows. 'It was always very important to the Venetians,' she explained, 'to be rich and have fun.'

The very least you can do, if you are not booked into a ball and don't want to splash out on a costume, is to wear a mask. As one local explained, 'It will give you the possibility of being more than you are… someone liberated. It will let you be a child again in a life which has so much responsibility.'

Mine's now back home, sitting on my mantlepiece, waiting for another opportunity for liberation.

32

LORDS OF THE RING

No matter how well you know London, however many years you may have lived there, the Capital Ring that circumnavigates the city will be a revelation. Or rather, a series of amazing revelations. Walking the entire route, of around eighty well-signposted miles, broken into seven- or eight-mile sections, I saw a London I barely knew existed.

Access to the Capital Ring is made easy by taking advantage of the 'hub and spoke' nature of the city's transportation system, which is primarily designed to feed commuters into the middle of town from the outer 'burbs. In practice, this means that you can join a sector of the route by taking a spoke from home to the bullseye, then another out to the Ring, returning at the end of the day's walking by a different spoke. For the next outing you simply go back to where your last leg finished.

Another essential aid is a good guide book, namely *The Capital Ring* by Colin Saunders, which includes not only detailed maps but lots of interesting information about sights to be seen along the way.

What follows is a day-by-day journal of my walk. Aside from the guide book, I had other companions. One, Geoff Dobson, aka Lord of the Ring Number Two, joined me for the entire walk. We also had a number of different joiners, a mix of friends and family members who accompanied us on some of the individual sectors.

Enough of the background. On with the show…

January 10: Green Ways

We began our walk at the end of my road, at Highgate tube station. It was a beautiful winter's morn, crispy cold but with a fierce sun dead ahead. We had to squint and shield our eyes to read the signposts.

For starters, we followed the raised embankment known as the Parkland Walk, built to carry a tube line that never happened. It was conceived to link Finsbury Park with Alexander Palace and on up to Edgware, following the track of the nineteenth-century railway line which was axed in the fifties. It's now an official nature reserve and the longest linear park in London, popular with joggers, cyclists, dog walkers and the occasional Capital Ringer.

The green theme continued through Finsbury Park and along the bank of what looked like a skinny canal but in fact was an ambitious engineering work designed to bring fresh water from a spring in Hertfordshire, some forty miles away, dropping a mere inch every half a mile.

We passed a pair of reservoirs, one a nature reserve, the other devoted to water sports. Ahead lay the castellated Rumpelstiltskin of a tower, an old water pumping station that is now an indoor climbing centre. This was still home turf London for both of us. We went past a flat where I used to live and, in Clissold Park, Geoff pointed to a bench where he took a break from the hospital bedside after the birth of his first child.

We stopped for soup in the cafe in Clissold Park, a perfect pit stop in a rather grand house, packed with mums and babes. We discussed last Saturday's football results, Geoff being a Spurs fan, me an Arsenal, but here we are, sharing our version of a London Derby but with no signs of tribal conflict (though it was still early days…).

A final leg took us along Stoke Newington High Street, past the house where Daniel Defoe lived (marked with a blue plaque), and into the eerie Albany cemetery, thick with teetering, ornate tombs and matted vegetation. It was a fitting end to the day's walk which was just the beginning of our journey – for us that is, not for the 300,000 poor souls who lay beneath the frosted earth.

January 16: The Lea of the Land

The Lords set off from where they'd left off, Stoke Newington station, and promptly took a wrong turn. I recalled a quote from Daniel Boone who, when asked if he'd ever been lost on all his travels, remarked, 'Nope, but I was a mite confused once for three days.' But our confusion lasted less than three minutes and, with a quick flick of the inner rudder, we were back on course. The weather was cold but a threatening pewter cloud was thankfully brushed aside by the biting breeze.

After the first few residential streets, peopled by an interesting and seemingly harmonious mix of orthodox Jews and Muslims, we entered Springfield Park, famous for its 'Two Giants', a pair of centenarian beech trees, and a sweeping view across the Lea Valley. We followed the river Lea, which flows all the way from the Chilterns to the Thames, its banks lined with traditional canal boats, several in a poor state of maritime health, but many being permanent homes with smoke puffing from inner wood stoves.

After 'Ackney 'Enge, the local version of Stonehenge, named after a cluster of concrete plinths that once supported a pumping engine, there was a distinct, socio-economic uplift, the moored boats in better nick, the bank-side properties smarter. The last stretch of the day followed the Greenway, aka the Northern Outfall Sewage Embankment (NOSE for short!), whose hidden pipe works daily carry 100 million gallons of unmentionables for processing before being dumped in the Thames. We heard no underground rumblings, nor caught any nasty whiffs.

This whole area was London as a work in progress, a combination of desolate wasteland and weedy, general scrappiness, but populated by platoons of men in hi-vis orange and lime greens looking like Playmobil figures and lots of heavy plant in construction choreography.

Our route passed close to the massive Olympic stadium, the Anish Kapoor spiralling tower and the aquatics centre designed by Zaha Hadid to look like a gentle ocean swell. In hindsight, we should have taken swimming gear and gone for a few fifty-metre laps in the beautiful Olympic pool.

Time to refuel. We stopped at an excellent, daffodil-yellow cafe called Moka East, assembled from old ship containers overlooking the stadium, and tucked into an excellent 'Have It All' ciabatta stuffed with egg, sausage, bacon and mushroom. This chapter ended with a ride into town by DLR from nearby Pudding Mill Lane station.

January 31: A Temple to Sewage

So, back to Pudding Mill Lane and to meet Mick Gardiner, a third Lord. A one-day peerage, you might say. Actually, perhaps a joiner should hold lesser ranks: a Baron, perhaps? The three of us spent a few minutes in joint conversation, by which I mean talking about knee joints, hips, quadriceps tendons, etc. Typical codger chat.

And then we were off, returning to the Greenway, soon to pass an amazingly ornate Victorian building, known as the 'Temple of Sewage', but now disused, abandoned and protected by a nasty-looking fence topped by razor wire.

Most of the walk was dead straight and rather boring but with a few distractions, such as the line which divides the western and eastern hemispheres. Unlike Greenwich, which bigs up the geographical significance, there's not even a 'Zero Meridian' information board. Without the trusted guide book, we would have stepped right over it.

A Porsche showroom on the fringes of Stratford seemed a sure sign of the neighbourhood's changing fortunes. We also saw an Alp, the name given to a huge slag heap created by the old Becton gas works, now coated by a dry ski slope.

At Becton we crossed the busy six-lane A13 by footbridge and took to the streets before turning into the pleasant Becton Park. The wavy route through the greenery, the first and only swathe of lushness all day, led more or less all the way to the Royal Albert Dock and City airport, where we 'I Spied' different aircraft liveries.

February 6: Lows and Highs

We decided to tackle two sectors of the route on the same day. Boy, the boys must be getting in shape.

The day was gloriously sunny so we set off through the playing fields, past a 'trotting track' which we figured was for horses rather than bionic walkers, and on through the campus of the University of East London. Set on the banks of the mile-long stretch of the Royal Albert Dock, its students are housed in a row of architecturally impressive halls of residence. Maybe the waterscapes could prove a little too distracting for serious study, not to mention interruptions from the roar of aircraft taking off from City airport on the far bank.

The Albert and neighbouring George V formed part of the Royal Docks which, though hard to imagine today, were not so long ago the largest in the world. My own grandfather was a stevedore somewhere here but it seems a shame that there isn't even a crane left as a memorial (not to him, but to mercantile heritage in general). There is one historic building, however, the Listed Galleons Hotel, where passengers about to embark on liners to the new world would stay before sailing.

After a nondescript stretch of road we reached the north bank of the Thames, an exciting moment despite the riverside path here being rather grim and neglected. Sights include the spot where the effluent from the Greenway sewage pipes feeds into the river, and two mighty locks where ships would pass from the river into the docks (including, on one occasion, the 35,000-ton *Mauretania*). On the opposite bank stood the high risers of Thamesmead new town and the nineteenth-century Royal Arsenal, the munitions factory being the place where the first football players worked. I thought the present day team still deserved to be called 'Royal' but Geoff took issue with that.

The end of the first stage was the Woolwich foot tunnel, a white-tiled pedestrian tube, a third of a mile long, that took us under the river, sixty feet below sea level and the lowest point of the Capital Ring. The lift wasn't working so we took the 126 steps down, taking heed of the large notice at the entrance forbidding 'cycling, busking, animal fouling, littering, loitering, skateboarding, skating and spitting'.

The Woolwich free ferry also shuttles to and from here, a voyage that the skippers must find both challenging (tides, river traffic, tricky docking manoeuvres, etc.) and boring, neither port of call offering anything like the excitement of a sea-going passage. There's been a river crossing here since the twelfth century.

We followed the south bank, our route now married to three others, the official Thames Path, the Jubilee Greenway and the National Cycle Network. An M1 for the self-propelled, you might say. The new iconic London landmarks, including Canary Wharf, the O2 and the Thames Barrier, lay ahead. We passed the site and remnants of the old Royal Navy dockyard where King Henry VIII's *Great Harry*, the largest warship ever built, rolled down the slipway in 1512, followed 300 years later by Darwin's *Beagle*.

The route soon parted company with the river and followed a mix of road and a corridor of green embedded in the urban sprawl of Charlton. We also kept company with the Green Chain Walk, firstly through an undulating landscape of old sand pits, then past a pen of deer in a children's zoo.

We later embarked on one of the most attractive sections of the entire way, beginning with Eltham Common, then into delightful ancient woodlands, up to Severndroog Castle, a gothic folly on top of Shooters Hill, the highest point in the entire walk (sharing the day with the lowest).

The castle, erected in memory of the Indian exploits of an eighteenth-century military man and local laird, Commodore Sir William James, was open for views, teas and wees.

The last half hour or so comprised more grand views, lots of woods and a short dog leg to Falconwood station, where we caught one of the frequent trains to London. We had reached the most easterly point of the Capital Ring, and with eleven miles under our belts, we both fell asleep on the train.

February 20: Ladies of the Ring

Our companions for this day were our wives, Charlotte and Monica, mine and his, a frequent 'drinks and eats' foursome but this was our first active outing. It was especially interesting to see the Capital Ring through fresh eyes and to understand their surprise at how remarkably rural London can be. The day's greenery included a riding stable, farmland, a field full of donkeys, a cemetery, golf course, football pitches, woodlands, Kent County Cricket Ground and, in the wake of heavy rain the previous days, a lot of squelchy mud, ideal for perfecting Torvill and Dean moves.

The first clue to the day's iconic highlight was a Tudor brick structure covering a sluice that regulated the flow of water to, cue fanfares, Eltham Palace. The grand building seen today is not the one which, from the early fourteenth century, reigned as the monarch's prime residence (until Henry VIII shunned it in favour of Hampton Court). Today's building was the creation of the Courtauld textile family and contains some of the best examples of Art Deco in the country.

Those craving for more historic authenticity, and fans of *Wolf Hall*, have only to look at the half-timbered building next door, home to both Cardinal Wolsey and Sir Thomas Moore.

Soon after there were grand panoramas of the London skyline to behold, a broad sweep spanning the O2 to the Shard. Towards the end of the day the path followed a wavy course through Beckenham Place Park and up to the Palladian mansion of Beckenham Place.

February 27: Walking with Dinosaurs

Our plus one for this day's walk was mutual pal Paul Gogarty (sixty plus – but not the dinosaur mentioned above). Unfortunately, the sector had rather an excess of tarmac until right at the end, so I'm going to fast track to Crystal Palace.

This great swathe of greenery, topped by its famous TV mast, the eighth-tallest structure in London, also includes the National Sports Centre and the scant remains of the old glass structure designed by Paxton for the Great Exhibition of 1851 but which was destroyed by fire in 1936. Six million people came, a third of the entire population of Britain.

To the dinosaurs, huge sculptures created in the 1850s beside a series of lakes. I last admired them some sixty years ago when I came with my dad. I still have the tiny black and white photo of the same beasts, taken with my old box camera. A strange feeling.

March 27: Gateway to the South

Today we walked a leg and a half, from the Palace to Balham. Every time any oldie hears that name he invariably recalls the comic track from the album *Songs for Swinging Sellers* in which, in a mockumentary extolling the virtues of the suburb, Sellers calls it the 'Gateway to the South'. Hilarious. Well, we thought so.

The day's highlights included Norwood Grove, better known as the White House, built by Arthur Anderson, the MP for the Shetland Isles and founder of the Peninsula & Orient shipping line. It presides on top of a hill, surrounded by fine gardens.

Other architectural gems of the day included a glorious, late nineteenth-century temple topped by a cupola, another of the Ring's grand water pumping stations. We also had a side-on glimpse of Tooting Bec Lido, which has one of the biggest pools in Europe, 100 yards long by thirty-three wide. We awarded our green gong of the day to the beautifully landscaped Rookery on Streatham Common, with exotic blooms, a massive cedar, ornamental pond, a rock and walled garden.

We stopped for a light bite at the San Remo Cafe beside the entrance, overlooking Streatham Common. A Sicilian girl took our order, first Geoff's whose request for a 'tuna' panini arrived as 'two' panini, reminiscent of the classic *Two Ronnies* sketch in the hardware store when Barker asks Corbett for 'fork handles' and gets 'four candles'. Or was it the other way round? We then ordered two teas. Geoff's arrived first, a cup of milk without a teabag. Can't be much call for builders' tea in Palermo, we surmised.

April 4: Deer Departed

Another day for the Lords and their Ladies, an eleven-miler from Balham to Richmond, a sector of the Ring which we later rated as the most stunning.

On Wandsworth Common we first walked beside a Giverny-ish pond, guarded by an enormous heron, the pastoral bliss coming to an abrupt halt at the imposing hulk of Wandsworth Prison. It looked impossible to get in, let alone out, although it did manage to lose Ronnie Biggs in 1965 (Biggs stars in another back story on page 150). Oscar Wilde was also incarcerated here, as was Derek Bentley, who was hanged for the murder of a police officer. It was a crime he did not commit, a travesty of justice and a most convincing argument against capital punishment.

We walked beside the well-tended graves in Wandsworth Cemetery, crossed the River Wandle, one of the Thames' many tributaries, and entered Wimbledon Park. With the stands of the All England Lawn Tennis and Croquet Club close by, we detoured to look at a lake, part of the grand design by 'Capability' Brown (who, I'm ashamed to say, I'd always assumed was a woman until I saw the memorial bust). Just outside the park we passed a number of practice courts which could well be a clever place to watch the Wimbledon pros warm up without having to pay for a ticket.

After crossing the busy A219 we stepped into the woods of Putney Heath, the beginning of a virtually unblemished stretch of parkland. We stopped, and would heartily recommend, the cafe by the Windmill for lunch before marching forth. Passing and crossing the fairways of the London Scottish Golf Club, where red tops are compulsory (shirts, not their daily tabloids), the route crosses the Kingston Bypass and enters Richmond Park.

The seventeenth-century hunting grounds of Charles I encompass some 2,500 acres grazed by 600-plus deer, none of which we managed to spot. It also houses the White Lodge which now belongs to the Royal Ballet School. After a kink to the left through Sidmouth Wood and one to the right into Petersham Park, we came upon Pembroke Lodge, the childhood home of Bertrand Russell and now the perfect spot for a tea break. Close by, and marked on the OS map, is the mound where Henry VIII stood in 1536 looking for a signal from the Tower of London that would confirm that Anne Boleyn's head had been successfully severed.

Leaving the park, we cut across Petersham Meadows, famously painted by Turner, for a stretch besides the Thames where the Capital Ring marries the Thames Path. The final leg ran the gauntlet of shops to Richmond Station and a choice of underground or overground homewards.

May 11: Waterways

Another glorious day, just Geoff and I in what seemed like the first showing of summer. It was also the first 'outing' of the year for four bare legs, still bleached winter white below the hem of our shorts.

Back to the Thames, passing the Old Deer Park before crossing the bridge to the opposite bank at Richmond lock and weir. At Isleworth Ait, meaning island, we enjoyed a wholly natural reach of riverbank whose muddy shores, the notice board explained, is home to freshwater shrimp and the 'German Hairy Snail'.

Geoff lagged behind at this point, fascinated by a pair of necking swans whose courtship he captured on camera, while I waited at the gates to Syon Park. Although barely into the day's mileage, which we reckoned could well top eleven plus as we were intent on stitching together two sectors from the guide book, we stopped for a sandwich in the sun at the Syon Park Garden Centre Refectory.

The Robert Adam designed Syon House, another landscaped by 'Capability' Brown, is the London pied a terre of the Dukes of Northumberland. The 'Syon', once a convent named after Jerusalem's Mount Zion, was dissolved by Henry VIII. His funeral entourage paused here en-route to Windsor. By a twist of fate, his coffin supposedly burst open and parts of his body were eaten by dogs.

Aside from greenery, a defining theme of the day was water. Having parted company with the Thames, we were soon following the banks of the River Brent and the towpath of the Grand Union Canal, a linear oasis bordered by commercial edifices including the enormous, glass-walled GlaxoSmithKline pharmaceutical giant. It was noisy hereabouts, with traffic on the Great West Road (the A4), then the Piccadilly Line and the M4, yet the Ring stubbornly refused to be side-tracked, ploughing forth over and under bridges.

After passing under the M4 we came across a plaque commemorating a British Waterways' team success in a 1959 'pile driving' competition. After passing through the six impressive locks of the 'Hanwell Flight', the canal leaves the river and continues to Birmingham – so we made sure not to take a wrong turn.

We walked beneath Brunel's viaduct, built to carry the Great Western railway over the river valley, and followed its meanders through Brent Lodge Park, detouring to tackle its maze before heading home.

June 19: Twin Peaks

'Welcome to Greenford,' said the uniformed Underground station attendant as we passed through the ticket barrier. What a wonderful, never heard before, and probably never again, greeting from a TFL official. Maybe visitors here are an endangered species? But whatever the reason, his words were greatly appreciated. Encouraged by such Greenford hospitality, we decided to enjoy another at the corner bakery, a poshed-up workers' caff with first-class muffins, before setting off.

Most of the day's eight or so miles felt far more rural than urban. We followed the towpath of the Grand Union Canal, crossed meadows, walked through woods and beside nature reserves, and climbed Horsenden Hill for one of the grandest of the Ring's panoramas. The view was also being enjoyed by four elderly gents who wished us good day before continuing their discussion – on haemorrhoids! Another 'pile driving' competition, perhaps?

The day was also one of the hilliest on the Ring, with Harrow on the Hill another high point, topographically and demographically. The famous school, fees circa £35,000 pa, is both 'top notch and blue chip', according to the Good Schools' Guide, its alumni studded with prime ministers and royals.

We stopped for a snack at the Ballels Cafe des Arts in the heart of the old village, a delightful place with paintings and books to browse and such scholastic items on the menu as 'Bursars High Tea' and 'Master's Salad'.

Passing several school buildings and gaggles of boys in boaters, we stood at the furthest point of the Ring from central London, some ten miles from Charing Cross. On the far horizon stood the Shard and other high rises. I admit we felt rather smug about having, on our circumnavigation of the capital, walked on the 'other' side of those far away buildings.

We continued along Football Lane and across the school's playing fields, an amazing spread of pitches, twenty-four tennis courts and its sixty-acre farm.

The official end of this 6.2-mile section of the walk was South Kenton tube but, since we wanted this to be the penultimate journey, we felt we ought to chip off a mile or so of the final section, our last hurrah, rather than arrive home in grunts of exhaustion. So, we pressed on, and up, through Fryent Country Park to a pond at the summit of Barn Hill. From here we left the main route, dropped down along a path, then a road leading to Wembley Park station right beside the entrance to the stadium.

July 27: Home Run

Having spent the last few months seeing London from an almost entirely fresh perspective, and covering over seventy miles in the process, it was peculiar to be walking back not only to where we started but almost to my back garden, which backs onto the path through Highgate Wood.

We first followed the route through fields of hay, soon to be scythed and fed to horses at nearby stables. We swapped meadows for woodlands and picked up an old pilgrim's route that once led to the shrine of St Alban. We climbed to the summit of Gotfords Hill for more sweeping views, taking in the spire of St Mary's church, a previous touchpoint at Harrow on the Hill.

In the run up to the M1 the path runs along the bank of the mile-long Brent Reservoir, also known as the White Harp, built to feed water into the Regent's Canal but now a popular boating spot where day-glo coloured sails flit about like butterflies. Real butterflies also abound in the designated nature reserve, as well as some 200 recorded species of moth and 250 of bird.

The final approaches were mostly, sadly, rather urban, including a crossing of the country's M1 aorta and a section right beside the six-lane madness of the North Circular. There was a thin artery of green fringing, the Dollis Valley Greenwalk, but we both thought it a shame that the Capital Ring could not have encompassed Hampstead Heath.

As we passed behind my back garden, I must confess I was tempted to call it a day, some 400 yards short of Highgate Station, but Geoff, quite rightly, insisted we walk through the woods to the tube entrance. There we congratulated each other before hopping on a 134 bus back to my house and a celebratory glass of bubbly.

33

TRAVEL MOMENTS

WHAT A BORE

The Bay of Fundy on Canada's east coast has the highest tides on Earth, with a range that can exceed fifty feet. Riding its bore, which heralds the arrival of as many as 150 billion tonnes of water that floods into the bay with each incoming tide, is one of North America's most exhilarating adventures.

Wearing lifejackets over our swimwear, we poodle along the shallow, still water of the rusty red Shubenacadie River in an inflatable Zodiac. Our guide beaches it on a sandbank and we wait, watching a host of bald eagles soar majestically overhead, waiting for the fish that will be tossed around by the incoming water. After a few idle minutes, we hear a distant, almost a whispered roar, and are summoned back into the boat.

Some two hundred yards or so downstream we spot a seemingly insignificant-looking wave approaching, getting ever bigger and louder. Our guide points the boat directly at the cliff face of the bore which grows to around ten feet tall. We hit it, full on, shooting up and into the foaming frenzy. We shriek and scream as we ride the roller-coaster waves that follow in its wake, the boat sometimes disappearing completely from sight beneath our bodies.

As the full force of the bore begins to subside, we roll from the boat into the river and are carried downstream at a high speed until the guide hauls us back on board.

Boring? You've got to be kidding.

PEAK PERFORMER

We were trekking in Nepal, a small group accompanied by a platoon of porters and sherpas. While we spent the days walking, along broad, well-trodden and not too demanding gradients, our supporting cast would pack up the campsite, including the kitchen, dining tent, showers and loos, and load it onto their backs. Sometime, in the middle of the morning, they would scamper past us, wearing flip flops and bent under their loads weighing as much as fifty kilos while we huffed along like heritage steam locos.

One morning, at first light, I emerged from my tent and stood transfixed by a single, beautiful pink cloud that stood alone, high in the sky, above the duvet of early mist. It had clearly caught the first rays of the sun that had yet to rise above our horizon. One of the sherpas, who came over to bring me a mug of steaming black tea, followed my gaze. 'That cloud is amazing,' I remarked. 'Ah, yes, but, sir, it is not a cloud. It is the summit of a mountain.' That single image was enough to convey the incredible scale and soaring heights of the Himalayas.

LEOPARD TRACKS

One of the most exhilarating moments I've ever experienced on a safari was not seeing a magnificent herd of elephants, a pride of lions on the hunt or a pod of hippos bellowing in a lagoon. In fact, it did not involve a single animal sighting. One morning, soon after dawn, I had set off with a Kenyan guide in the hopes of spotting a leopard that had been seen, the previous afternoon, close to the lodge. He carried a rifle, just in case. We soon picked up fresh tracks and followed them, walking stealthily through a mix of scrub and woodland. Crouching through some low-hanging branches, we came across a patch of grass, shaped like a large, softly curved bowl. 'Just touch it with the palm of your hand,' my companion whispered. It was eerily warm to the touch. Slowly, almost imperceptibly, blades of flattened grass began to rise from the ground. The leopard had left the spot only moments before we arrived. We continued our tracking but never saw the animal.

ROYAL ENCOUNTER

When I was a very small boy, my parents took me to watch a polo match being played in Cowdray Park in West Sussex. My mum was particularly excited as the Duke of Edinburgh was expected to be riding. She spotted a make-shift notice board, stuck on a pole beside the playing field, and we went to take a closer look. A sheet of paper, pinned to the board, listed the order of play and each of the team members. We were excited to see that the Duke was down for a chukka or two at 4pm. As we studied the fixtures, just the two of us with nobody else around, a man came striding up to the board and quickly scanned the sheet. It was the Duke. 'Damn,' he said, obviously unhappy with the timings or the choice of playmates. 'Aaahhh,' said my mum, the sort of sound usually reserved for the first sight of a newly born kitten or puppy.

That, for the record, is the only exchange of words that has ever taken place between a member of my family and a Royal.

FINAL ASCENTS

The epithets at the end of two walking holidays share an uncanny similarity.

One marked the end of a week spent in Tuscany, walking between medieval hilltop towns that, by definition, meant a tough uphill slog at the end of a long day. On my last day I spotted Siena, our final night's stop, several hours before arriving, its Torre di Mangia, the tallest structure in the medieval world, still dominating the horizon like a homing beacon. The day's quota of a dozen or so hot miles came to a cruel end in a long crescendo of a hill. I skirted the magnificent Piazza del Campo and used my last drop of fuel in getting to the hotel, the Antico Torre. 'I have given you room 128, the *camera ultima*,' said the owner, pointing to a flight of stairs as narrow as a drinking straw.

There were fifty-six exhausting, just about manageable steps to my room. But what a garret! I opened the shutters and there, across a sea of lichen-crusted terracota tiles and through a flurry of chattering swifts, lay the countryside I had just walked. It was the landscape captured by the Renaissance masters.

My other bookend to a week's walking took place in Switzerland which, my wife and I concluded, was much more of an uphill country than a downhill one whichever direction you travel. Were it to be ironed flat, we pondered, would it spread as broad as, say, Germany? Maybe even Australia. One late afternoon, after we seemed to go up and up from inside the village of Chinois Brel, the river Inn far below like a scratch on the green valley meadows and communities looking like model villages we arrived in Zuoz. We felt and obviously looked exhausted when we finally checked into the Hotel Engiadina because the receptionist, when handing over the key to our room just on the first floor, unhesitatingly suggested we took the lift.

FISHY BUSINESS

I once spent three days in Lille as a guest of the local tourist office in order to write a city guide for the *Sunday Times*. The woman, Isabelle, who ran the office, invited me to dinner in L'Huitriere, which was part wet-fish shop in the front and an excellent, one-star Michelin seafood restaurant in the back. The meal was superb, particularly the main dish, which was cod. I recommended both the dish and the restaurant in the article.

Several months later I went back to Lille with my wife, just for the weekend. I tried to book L'Huitriere but could only get an answerphone message, which I didn't understand. I called Isabelle and asked whether she would do me a favour and make the booking on my behalf, explaining that it was a purely private visit, and I emphasised that I would be paying the bill. She booked a table, called me back to confirm and wished us 'bon appetit'.

The owner, monsieur Baillieul, welcomed us and, obviously tipped off by Isabelle, thanked me for the article which had appeared a few weeks prior to this second visit. I said I hoped the recommendation had brought one or two readers. 'But, monsieur Wickers,' he explained. 'It brought me many customers. And when they come, they always ask for the cod. But I often do not have the cod on the menu. Oh, they say. But we were told to have the cod. Some even bring the page from the newspaper and show me where it says they must have the cod.'

Sadly, the restaurant has since closed.

HOME HOSTS

I've stayed in many peculiar places over the years but one of the weirdest was a rather grand, private country house, somewhere in the home counties, that welcomed paying guests. At dinner the place reached a zenith of madness.

The meal was a pretentious, overly formal affair in which the owner, dressed in a tuxedo, hosted a table communally shared by around six or seven guests. Although he tried to structure a group bonding, by inviting each of the guests to comment on his chosen topic like a presenter on *Any Questions*, the effect was very unrelaxing. The atmosphere was made all the more uncomfortable by the woman who served us. She didn't say a word, her manner as rigid as if she were waiting at a Heads of State dinner at Buckingham Palace.

I'm sure we were all equally relieved when, after the dessert, our host explained how he would be taking his leave and, if we would care to make our way into the drawing room, his wife would be delighted to join us for coffee.

We filed out into the adjacent room where, sitting in a large, upright chair, sewing an embroidery sampler, a small Pekinese dog on her lap, was the 'waitress,' reincarnated as our hostess for the rest of the evening. 'Good evening, good evening,' she greeted us. 'Do help yourselves to café et petit fours,' she suggested, 'and do please tell me all about your delicious dinner and the fun I'm sure you had.'

A SANDALS LEGEND

Today (January 5, 2021) I read of the death of 'Butch' Stewart, the larger-than-life Jamaican who founded the hugely successful Sandals resorts in the Caribbean. I particularly remember him as someone who had the knack of making you feel far more important than you deserved.

I once interviewed him in his offices in Miami. He was welcoming, friendly and charming, and even happy to field questions about the negative impact of all-inclusive resorts on local economies.

The interview over, he graciously walked with me out of his office and into the foyer where the receptionist had just picked up a telephone call. 'Excuse me, Mr Stewart, but the

Prime Minister of Jamaica would like to have a word with you.' Without breaking his stride, Butch turned to her and said, 'Tell him I'm with David Wickers and I'll call him back in ten minutes.' To this day I'm still not sure whether the call was genuine, but it sure made me feel good.

WORKING HARD FOR THE MONEY

Ever since the sixties, Les Caves du Roy has been the hottest nightclub in St Tropez, attracting celebrities – Jack Nicholson to Lady Gaga – and the super-rich. The subterranean Caves belongs to the equally fashionable Byblos Hotel, where I once spent a night courtesy of its manager, Sylvain Ercoli, whom I had previously met during his reign as the GM at the swish Martinez Hotel in Cannes. After a late dinner, he and I visited the club, fast-tracking the entry line and straight past the bouncers, who gave us a polite *'bienvenue messieurs'*.

We stepped into a full on, dance-frenetic, pulsating party. Sylvain led me straight into a small, roped-off VIP section, where I was introduced to Joan Collins and friends. Someone offered me a glass of Cristal champagne. Sylvain asked if I would like to say 'hi' to the resident DJ in his eyrie above the dance floor, who greeted me warmly and asked if I'd like to choose the next track. I looked down on the action below, to the sea of beautiful boppers, and suggested Donna Summer's 'She Works Hard for the Money', which was the most incongruous choice I could possibly have made. None of the girls, many dancing on the table-tops, seemed to pick up on the irony.